EZEKIEL

By

RALPH ALEXANDER

MOODY PRESS

CHICAGO

© 1976 by
THE MOODY BIBLE INSTITUTE
OF CHICAGO
Second Printing, 1976

Library of Congress Cataloging in Publication Data

Alexander, Ralph.
  Ezekiel.
  Bibliography: p. 160.
  1. Bible, O. T. Ezekiel—Commentaries. I. Title.

BS1545.3.A43   224'.4'07   75-45234

ISBN 0-8024-2026-5

Printed in the United States of America

CONTENTS

CHAPTER   PAGE

Introduction   5

Outline   7

1. Yahweh's Commission of Ezekiel (1:1—3:27)   9

2. The Disobedience of Judah and Her Predicted Judgment
   (4:1—24:27)   20

3. The Sins of the Nations and Their Resulting Judgment
   (25:1—33:20)   80

4. The Faithfulness of God and Judah's Future Blessings
   (33:21—48:35)   104

   Blessings (33:21—48:35)   104

   Appendix: Cubit Measurements   159

   Bibliography   160

ILLUSTRATIONS

FIGURE   PAGE

1. Temple Complex   139

2. Gate System for All Gates of the Outer Court   141

3. The Plan of the Temple Sanctuary   143

4. Altar of Sacrifice   148

5. Land Allotment in the Millennium   152

To

Mother and Dad
whose love, training, and encouragement
enabled me to accomplish this task

INTRODUCTION

AUTHORSHIP AND DATE

The author of this prophecy has been traditionally recognized as Ezekiel, a priest and prophet who lived in the seventh and sixth centuries B.C. Ezekiel was taken to Babylon with the deportation of Jehoiachin in 597 B.C. One of the most complete chronological systems in any book of the Old Testament is found in this prophecy, demonstrating that Ezekiel's ministry covered at least the span of 593 to 571 B.C. Only recently have these factors been questioned by critics. The most radical objections came from C. C. Torrey in 1930. Basic criticisms fall in two essential areas: (1) the failure to understand how Ezekiel could pronounce judgment and blessing in the same book; and (2) the fact that portions of his prophecies seem to be written by one residing in Judah, not Babylon.

Lack of understanding the role of the prophets lies behind the first objection. Each of the prophets was acting in the role of a prosecuting attorney in the indictment of Israel for breaking the Mosaic covenant. All they could offer from that covenant was cursing because Israel had broken the Law. Yet the eternal Abrahamic and Davidic covenants gave the prophets a basis for announcing the hope of restoration. The second criticism refuses to understand the visionary nature of many of Ezekiel's messages. He was not present in Israel; he was transported in visions by the Holy Spirit to perceive what was transpiring in Judah.[1]

EZEKIEL AND THE HISTORICAL CONTEXT

Ezekiel was both a priest and a prophet. He ministered at the end of the surviving kingdom of Judah when Judah was vacillating between dependence on Egypt and Babylon for her existence. With the death of

1. For fuller discussions of authorship and date, cf. Hobart E. Freeman, *An Introduction to the Old Testament Prophets,* pp. 299-302, and Gleason L. Archer, Jr., *A Survey of Old Testament Introduction,* rev. ed., pp. 369-73.

Josiah, first Egypt and then Babylon, gained control of the small nation of Judah. In 597 B.C. Nebuchadnezzar attacked Jerusalem, plundered the city, and deported the king, Jehoiachin, and many others to Babylon. Ezekiel was deported at this time and took up residence at Tel-Abib beside the river Chebar along with the majority of the exiles. In Jehoiachin's place, Nebuchadnezzar established Zedekiah on the throne of Judah. He ultimately rebelled, precipitating the final fall of Jerusalem in 586 B.C. (cf. 2 Ki 23:28—25:30; 2 Ch 35:20—36:23). While in captivity, Ezekiel received his commission from Yahweh at the age of thirty. His messages date from 593 to 571 B.C.

SUMMARY OF THE BOOK

Ezekiel wrote his messages to the exiles in essentially a chronological order. He, as a watchman, warned Judah that her disobedience to the Mosaic covenant would bring its cursing upon her in the form of judgment upon the land and upon Jerusalem. Ezekiel employed every means to communicate his message: speaking, acting, visions, symbols, allegories, parables. But Judah had gone too far; Yahweh's glory was removed from the Temple and from Judah in preparation for the coming judgment. Systematically Ezekiel removed all of the contemporary arguments against such a judgment. Then Jerusalem fell. Quickly judgment was also announced on the nations around Judah who cheered at her collapse and sought to plunder her.

The final portion of the book brought hope. Just prior to the reception of the news of Jerusalem's fall by the exiles in Babylon, Ezekiel received and proclaimed six night messages of blessing on Judah through cleansing and restoration to the land of Israel in the Millennium. With the return of Israel to her land, Yahweh's glory would return to the new Temple constructed as His dwelling place among them.

6

OUTLINE

I. YAHWEH'S COMMISSION OF EZEKIEL (1:1—3:27).

   A. The Vision of the Glory of God (1:1—2:2).

   B. Recipients of Ezekiel's Message (2:3—3:14).

   C. Ezekiel's Charge (3:15-27).

II. THE DISOBEDIENCE OF JUDAH AND HER PREDICTED JUDGMENT (4:1—24:27).

   A. The Watchman's Initial Warning of Judgment (4:1—7:27).

   B. The Departure of the Glory of Yahweh from Jerusalem (8:1—11:25).

   C. Answers to the Exiles' False Optimism (12:1—19:14).

      1. Monodrama: Going into Exile (12:1-20).

      2. God's Judgment Viewed as Certain (12:21-28).

      3. Woe to the Prophets and Prophetesses (13:1-23).

      4. The Work of a True Prophet (14:1-11).

      5. The Righteous Able to Deliver Only Themselves (14:12-23).

      6. Israel: A Vine Fit Only for Burning (15:1-8).

      7. Jerusalem: The History of a Harlot (16:1-63).

      8. The Riddle and Allegory of Two Eagles (17:1-24).

      9. Each Man Seen as Living or Dying by His Own Deeds (18:1-32).

      10. A Dirge Against the Rulers of Judah (19:1-14).

   D. The History of Israel's Corrupt Leadership (20:1—23:49).

      1. The Past Corruption of Israel and Her Leadership (20:1-44).

      2. The Resulting Judgment on Contemporary Judah and Her Leadership (20:45—21:32).

      3. Vindication of Yahweh's Judgment upon the Leaders of Judah (22:1-31).

4. A Summary Parable of the Political Prostitution of the Nation Israel (23:1-49).

E. The Enactment of Jerusalem's Judgment (24:1-27).

III. THE SINS OF THE NATIONS AND THEIR RESULTING JUDGMENT (25:1—33:20).

A. The Judgment upon the Nations Immediately Surrounding Judah (25:1-17).

B. The Judgment upon Tyre and Sidon (26:1—28:26).

C. The Judgment upon Egypt (29:1—33:20).

IV. THE FAITHFULNESS OF GOD AND JUDAH'S FUTURE BLESSINGS (33:21—48:35).

A. Night Messages of Hope and Encouragement (33:21—39:29).
   1. Jerusalem Fallen; Separation from the Land (33:21-33).
   2. False Shepherds of Israel; the True Shepherd (34:1-31).
   3. Judgment of Possessors of the Land; Israel Again the Possessor (35:1—36:15).
   4. Restoration of the People of Israel to Their Land (36:16—37:14).
   5. The Reunion of Israel and the Fulfillment of Her Covenants (37:15-28).
   6. The Final Attempt of Foreigners to Possess the Land of Israel (38:1—39:29).

B. The Return of the Glory of God (40:1—48:35).
   1. The Setting of the Apocalyptic Vision (40:1-4).
   2. The Content of the Apocalyptic Vision (40:5—48:35).
      a. The description of the millennial Temple area (40:5—42:20).
      b. The portrayal of the return of the glory of God to the Temple (43:1-9).
      c. The Temple regulations (43:10—46:24).
      d. The geographical characteristics of the land of Israel in the Millennium (47:1—48:35).

1

YAHWEH'S COMMISSION OF EZEKIEL

1:1—3:27

SUMMARY

To present a divine message, it is necessary for the messenger to understand the nature of God and His divine perspectives. Thus God revealed His glory to Ezekiel through a vision (1:1-28a) so that Ezekiel might thoroughly grasp the holiness, power, and wonder of a just, loving, and covenant God who was about to exhibit His faithfulness to His covenants with Israel through judgment and blessing. The Mosaic covenant was a conditional covenant. If the nation of Israel obeyed the stipulations of this treaty, she would appropriate the blessings of Yahweh, which were intimately connected to the possession of the land of Canaan and its fruitfulness. On the contrary, if the people disobeyed this Law, they would experience the cursing of God which would be manifested by their expulsion from Canaan and the desolation of the land (cf. Deu 27-28).

Ezekiel, a priest, knew the Law well. He also understood the condition of Israel; she had continually broken the Mosaic covenant. God had already begun to exercise His covenant judgment by removing Judah from Palestine through the Babylonian deportations in 605 and 597 B.C. Ezekiel was carried to Babylon in 597 B.C. The final destruction of Jerusalem and Judah could not be far off. It would be Ezekiel's task to announce it to the captives in Babylon. In order that he might be reminded that this was God's purpose and that He was just and righteous in exercising this discipline upon Israel, God revealed Himself in all His covenant glory to Ezekiel through a vision of symbols.

9

Having seen the glory of the covenant God, Ezekiel could more easily receive His commission. Yahweh charged him to go to the "house of Israel," the exiles who were already in captivity. These exiles, he was warned, would not be amenable to his message, for they were stubborn and impudent rebels against God, as had been the character of Israel from her inception. Though they would not want to listen, still Ezekiel must speak God's message, a task that would only be possible as he spoke in the authority of God. Then Israel would know that a prophet had been in her midst (1:28b—2:5).

Man is always concerned about how other men will react to his actions and words. Ezekiel was no exception. After all, had not God just declared that Israel would rebel and close her ears to the message he would deliver? Undoubtedly a quiver of fearful reticence and dismay pricked Ezekiel's heart. But God, knowing the natural resistance of man to the things of God, anticipated these anxieties by encouraging Ezekiel not to fear or to be dismayed, regardless of the hindrance and discomfort which might arise from opposition in Israel. He was exhorted to speak God's words, whether they wanted to listen or not (2:6-7).

God promised to give Ezekiel His words, for God never leaves His messenger without a message. But at the same time it was imperative that Ezekiel first hear and assimilate God's words, not his own. "Do not rebel against My word as Israel did," warns Yahweh, "but go and speak that which you receive from Me and thoroughly understand, a message of judgment" (see 2:8—3:3).

But, thinks Ezekiel, *they will not like that kind of message.* God agreed by stating that it would be easier to learn a foreign language and deliver this message to that foreign nation than to penetrate the stubborn deafness of Israel (3:4-7).

God, however, always equips His spokesman for the task to which He calls him. He gave Ezekiel the exact equipment which he would need to meet this challenge: a head that was harder than Israel's in order that he might be able to stand adamantly (3:8-11).

This was enough instruction for Ezekiel to meditate upon in one session. God did not overwhelm him with the entire commission in one sitting, but spread it out over a period of time. Therefore, this initial vision closes as the hand of Yahweh took him to Tel-Abib, the major settlement of the exiles. There, as Ezekiel mused on the vision, he had feelings of distress and anguish over announcing judgment upon his own people. However, he also had begun to sense the holiness and righteous anger of God. All of this caused him to sit overwhelmed, silently meditating on the task before him and consecrating himself to it. He, of all people, had to uphold God's covenant with Israel, and live and minister in light of it (3:12-15).

Having permitted Ezekiel the time to mull over His initial charge, Yahweh then spelled out his role more specifically. "Ezekiel," He said, "you know how a watchman of a city has the responsibility to warn its inhabitants of any impending danger from the external invasion of an enemy or internal riot or fire. You, too, will be a watchman, not to a city, but rather to a nation—Israel. You must warn them of the impending judgment of God which is on the horizon. If you warn them, and if they respond and turn to Me, they shall live. If you warn them, and they do not repent and therefore die, at least you have been responsible to your job. But if you fail to alert them of the coming judgment and they die as a result, you have committed murder and will be held responsible for the whole nation" (see 3:16-21).

Ezekiel was then led out on the plain to receive the last portion of his commission. Having reminded Ezekiel a second time that this was the work and charge of God through the vision of His glory, God announced the unique manner in which Ezekiel was to carry out his role as a watchman. He was to withdraw from the life of the exiles, obsessed with the impending judgment on Judah. Yahweh would cause Ezekiel to be dumb, except when He opened Ezekiel's mouth to proclaim God's messages (3:22-27).

THE VISION OF THE GLORY OF GOD
(1:1—2:2)

Symbolic dream-visions were common to the seventh and sixth century B.C. Mesopotamian culture in which the Israelite exiles found themselves.[1] It is not surprising therefore that God chose to reveal many of His messages during the captivity through this literary form, for the

---

1. A. Leo Oppenheim, *The Interpretation of Dreams in the Ancient Near East with a Translation of an Assyrian Dream-Book,* pp. 179-373.

Israelites most certainly were familiar with it. These dream visions contained two basic sections: (1) the setting of the vision, and (2) the vision proper.

The vision in chapter 1 of Ezekiel follows this pattern. The setting is given in the first three verses, with the usual information of date, place, recipient, and attending circumstances. The date is stated in two ways. First, it is the thirtieth year of Ezekiel's life. An Old Testament priest began his public ministry at the age of thirty (Num 4:23, 30, 39, 43), and Ezekiel was a priest (Eze 1:3). Second, the thirtieth year of Ezekiel's life was also the fifth year of the exile of King Jehoiachin from Jerusalem (2 Ki 24:10-16). Ezekiel was taken to Babylon in that deportation, and the events of his prophecy are all dated from that deportation of 597 B.C. (cf. Eze 40:1). This would specify the date of this vision as 593 B.C.[2]

The place where this vision was received was among the exiles on the river Chebar, a navigable canal of the Euphrates flowing southeast from Babylon in the land of Chaldea.

The recipient, Ezekiel, was the son of Buzi, of whom we know nothing. Ezekiel was declared to be a priest, which is extremely significant to the interpretation of this prophecy. He would look at Israel from a priestly perspective, and this, in turn, will constantly force the reader to turn back to the Mosaic covenant with its liturgical and priestly duties (Ex 20 through Deu).

The only attending circumstance mentioned in this setting is the hand of the Lord upon Ezekiel, demonstrating that the forthcoming vision is uniquely wrapped up in the purposes and work of God for Ezekiel.

The vision itself is recounted in 1:4-28a. The interpretations of this vision have often been fanciful, subjective, and confusing. Interpreters have become so engrossed in distinguishing and identifying details of the vision that they have often overlooked its major significance. Divine interpretations are given normally as an inherent part of the dream vision. Thus, it would seem prudent to follow the divine interpretation when it is given. Likewise, one should observe that the divine interpreta-

---

2. Cf. above in Introduction.

tions usually center on the major import of the vision rather than on details.[3]

When these basic interpretive principles are applied to the vision at hand, it immediately becomes obvious that the point of this vision is not as difficult as some have thought it to be; it portrays the "visions of God" (1:1) and "the appearance of the likeness of the glory of the LORD" (1:28). This, therefore, is a vision of the glory of God, a concept further supported by parallel passages within this book. In 3:12, 23-24 (still part of Ezekiel's commission), he recounted that he once again saw the glory of Yahweh, the same glory which he saw previously on the river Chebar when Yahweh spoke to him. Ezekiel mentioned this again when he saw a similar vision in 8:2-4; 10:1-2, 15-20; and 43:2-4. He was seeing again the vision of God's glory, the glory that appeared in the Holy of Holies of the Temple (Ex 25:15-18; 29:42-46; 40:34-38).

The dream-vision style of Mesopotamia described the recipient recounting exactly what he saw in the vision, often coupled with the "divine" interpretation. Ezekiel followed this pattern. The vision as a whole was perceived as a violent electrical storm from the north. Within the storm he observed two major objects: (1) four living creatures with attending wheels, and (2) one like a man enthroned upon an expanse stretching over the heads of the four living creatures.

Each of the four living creatures (1:4-14) had the likeness and the general appearance of a man within the bright glow of sparkling burnished bronze, lightning, and torches (1:4, 5, 7, 13, 14). Each creature had four faces (that of a man, lion, ox or cherub, and eagle), with the man's face being most prominent (cf. 1:6-10; 10:14, 22). The living being had four wings, two joined together and two covering the body (1:9, 11, 23). The wings had a sound like the voice of God when they flapped. Each living being had a man's hands under his wings, and straight legs with calf's soles. A high, frightful, whirling wheel, sparkling like a precious stone and full of eyes on its rim, stood next to each creature (cf. 10:2). The arrangement of the four wheels caused them

3. Ralph H. Alexander, "Hermeneutics of Old Testament Apocalyptic Literature" (Doctoral diss., Dept. of Semitics and O. T., Dallas Theol. Sem., 1968), p. 161.

to appear as if each wheel had a wheel in it. The movement of the living creatures and their wheels was coordinated. Together they moved as the spirit of the living creature directed (cf. 1:9, 12, 14, 17, 19-21). Coals of fire lay between these four living creatures (cf. 10:2, 7).

These living creatures were later identified by Ezekiel in chapter 10 as cherubim (cf. 10:20). Many argue that these cherubim formed a throne chariot upon which the glory of God rode (cf. Ps 18:10). There appears to be some substantiation of this in 1 Chronicles 28:18. Ezekiel, a priest, would be acquainted from his Temple training with cherubim over the Ark of the Covenant and those worked into the design of the veil (Ex 25:18-22; 26:31). Normally cherubim accompanied the manifestation of the glory of God. To say any more than that seems to be risky and speculative, since the divine interpreter does not do so. The cherubim are seemingly angelic creatures who escort the holiness and righteousness of God's glory.

The second major aspect of this vision of God's glory involved a "firmament" or "expanse" with the appearance of sparkling ice upon which there was a similitude of a throne with the likeness of a sapphire stone. The likeness of a man, sparkling like amber and possessing the appearance of the brightness of a burning fire and a rainbow, was seated upon this throne. He is declared to be the appearance of the glory of God (Eze 1:28), speaking with a great rumbling voice.

This vision, therefore, represented the majestic and awesome glory of God, a picture similar to that which was given at the very beginning of the nation (cf. Ex 19 and 24) and which continued to represent Yahweh even in Ezekiel's day. How appropriate that the same manifestation of God that occurred at the giving of the Mosaic covenant should appear when He executed the judgments and promises of that covenant to the people with whom the covenant was made. Certainly there are variations in the picture of God's glory throughout the Old Testament, yet that should not be a concern because God's glory has no limitations. One should not expect the theophanies of God always to be identical. Yet the similarity of the basic figure of God's glory pervades not only the Old Testament but also finds its likeness in the Revelation to John (Rev 4). Surely this common manifestation is to facilitate the ease with which the student of Scripture might be able to recognize the appearance of the glory of God throughout the Bible. Because of His holiness and righteousness, this glorious God must execute His promised judgment and discipline upon rebellious Israel.

This concept of the glory of God played a most important role in the whole thrust of Ezekiel's prophecy. God's glory began the message, showing the glorious God of judgment. God's glory was to reside in the Temple; but because of the discipline of Israel at that time through the Babylonian captivity, the glory of God would leave the Temple, Jerusalem, and Israel (cf. 8:8; 9:3; 10:4, 18, 19; 11:22-23). The glory of God will not return to the land of Canaan until God Himself restores Israel to the land in that ultimate time of blessing, the Millennium (cf. chaps. 43-44), when Jerusalem and the new Temple are rebuilt. This, therefore, provides the basic scheme of Ezekiel's message. It is from a priestly perspective. The glory of God which was over the cherubim in the Holy of Holies would leave because of judgment upon Israel, but it will return to its rightful place in the future restoration of Israel, according to the promises of the Mosaic covenant. Seeing God's glory, Ezekiel fell prostrate before God, as Israel should have done.

RECIPIENTS OF EZEKIEL'S MESSAGE
(2:3—3:14)

Those who were to hear the message of Ezekiel were the "children of Israel" (2:3), referred to literally in the Hebrew as "nations." One might immediately wonder how the nation of Israel could be referred to as nations, in the plural. This is more readily understood when the historical background is explained. With the death of Solomon (*c.* 931 B.C.) the nation of Israel split into two nations: the Northern Kingdom of Israel and the Southern Kingdom of Judah. With the deportation of the Northern Kingdom of Israel to Assyria in 722 B.C., the Southern Kingdom gradually became known again by the term Israel as well as by the name Judah. However, the reunion of the twelve tribes, or the two nations of Israel and Judah, began, it appears, in Babylon. This is what Ezekiel meant in reference to "nations" in the plural when speaking of the children of Israel in exile. The full and complete reunion of the two nations will take place in the final restoration of the end times (cf. 35:10; 36:13-15; 37:22).

The very use of the word "nation" pictures Israel as being regarded by God from the outside, rather than looking upon her more intimately as His "people" (cf. Ex 19:3-6; Deu 7:6-7). In no way, however, was God referring to His people as He would to Gentiles (*goyim,* Heb.), but He was making it clear that they were not acting like His covenant people.

The most frequently used phrase to describe the character of Ezekiel's audience is "a rebellious house." Nine times in Yahweh's commission to Ezekiel some form of the word "rebel" is used to depict Israel. The term implies bold and audacious acts of rebellion against Yahweh (2:3; 3:7). It manifests itself in the obstinance and impudence of these people. They were "hard-faced" and "strong-hearted," phrases employed to portray their stubborn, determined opposition to Yahweh and His message. They would refuse to listen to Yahweh (3:7) or Ezekiel, His messenger (2:5; 3:7, 11). Instead they would "prick" and "sting" Ezekiel like scorpions (2:6). They transgressed against Yahweh by refusing to subject themselves to His rightful authority as revealed in the Mosaic covenant. It would have been easier for Ezekiel to learn a foreign language and proclaim his message to a foreign people than to break through the obstinance of Israel (3:4-7).

This is a significant description of Israel, for here God set forth the reason for the judgment which Ezekiel would announce upon this people. *They had rebelled against God and broken His covenant.* This was not a recent development. It had been a characteristic of Israel from her birth (cf. 2:3 with Num 17:10; Deu 31:24-29; Pr 17:11; Is 30:8-14). Now the promise of discipline had arrived (Deu 29-30).

EZEKIEL'S CHARGE
(3:15-27)

God called Ezekiel to be a watchman to the house of Israel to warn them of the coming judgment (3:15-21). A watchman's task involved keeping a vigilant eye upon the horizon and upon the city itself to observe any dangers which might come to the town, whether from the enemy outside or from fire, riot, or disturbance within (cf. 2 Sa 18:24-27; 2 Ki 9:17-20). Ezekiel's main task as a watchman was to announce the imminent judgment of God upon Judah and Jerusalem, which was on the horizon. Just as the watchman of a city is liable when he fails to warn its inhabitants, so Ezekiel would be responsible if he failed to warn Isarel. If he warned the wicked one of the house of Israel that he would die, or the righteous one who turned from his righteousness that he would die, and they did not turn from their ways, and therefore died, Ezekiel had fulfilled his duty and was innocent of their death.

On the contrary, if he failed to warn the righteous or the wicked so that they likewise died, but without warning, then Ezekiel would be responsible for the spilling of their blood, and he would die ("their blood required at his hand"; cf. 2 Sa 4:5-12; Judg 9:24; and Eze 18, 33). The seriousness of his mission was clear. The false prophets who failed in their responsibility to warn Israel, but rather said "Peace" when there was no peace, suffered the consequences of God's judgment of death (cf. 13:1-23; 14:9-11).

Some have looked to this passage for support against the eternal security of the believer. The "righteous" man, they say, can turn from his righteousness and die an eternal death. It is necessary, however, that the reader understand the context of Ezekiel's writing and the usage of the term "righteous" in the Old Testament. Israel was supposed to *do* the righteousness contained in the principles of the Mosaic covenant (cf. Deu 16:20; 1 Sa 24:17; 1 Ki 8:32; Ho 14:9; Ps 119:7, 106, 121, 144, 160, 172; Is 58:2). To do all the stipulations of the Law was to be righteous and thereby to *live* in the land of promise (cf. Deu 6:25; 16:20). The Mosaic covenant pointed one to the Messiah and set forth a way of life for the believer in the Messiah through its commandments, but just the following of these commandments alone never gave anyone eternal life. Eternal righteousness and salvation are only by faith—a message proclaimed throughout the *entire* Scriptures. The "righteous" in this section was the believer in the Messiah who had been righteous in his following of the stipulations of the Mosaic covenant, but then turned from them. Ezekiel announced the judgment of God upon the nation of Israel because she had failed to keep the Mosaic covenant and thereby act righteously.

Ezekiel's message to the house of Israel may be concisely summarized as a warning of judgment, at least in the first twenty-four chapters of this book. It would consist of dirges, moanings, and lamentations (2:10) as well as a warning to listen and cease from iniquity (3:27). This was Yahweh's message and was to be communicated with God's authority (2:2-5, 7; 3:27). Ezekiel himself was cautioned not to rebel against the Lord's message as Israel would, but rather to hear it, accept it, and, having thoroughly understood it, to proclaim it whether or not Israel wanted to hear it (2:7—3:3, 10). By being required to eat the scroll upon which God's message was written, Ezekiel was demonstrating his acceptance of that message without alteration, as well as the necessity to completely assimilate God's message first before proclaiming it to His people. Even though it was a message of woe, because it was God's message, it was as sweet as honey (3:3).

God's statement to Ezekiel in 3:24-27 initially appears contradictory to the charge to warn the nation. How could Ezekiel be dumb, bound in his home, and not be a reprover to Israel if he was to be their watchman? Two items are involved: (1) the rejection he would receive from the exiles, and (2) the manner of his ministry as revealed by God. Verse 25 makes it very clear that the ones who would bind him and thereby cause him to be shut up in his home away from the people are "they," contextually the Jewish exiles. Verses 26-27 then declare that God would still work in this situation to use him in a unique way as a watchman.

Numerous explanations have been created to explain the prophet's dumbness. According to the rest of the prophecy, Ezekiel remained dumb for seven and one half years until the fall of Jerusalem (cf. 33:22). Yet, between chapters 3 and 33 Ezekiel uttered many messages (cf. 11:25; 14:1; 20:1). The solution lies in an understanding of his dumbness. When Ezekiel's total ministry is examined, the student sees that he never ministered in the streets and assemblies of the people as other prophets did. The normal prophet moved among his people, reacting to the issues of his day right on the spot. Not Ezekiel. He ministered through a strange immobility. The elders and people came to him to inquire from the Lord (cf. 8:1; 14:1; 20:1; 33:30-33), and then he spoke only when the Lord opened his mouth to proclaim, "Thus says the Lord GOD [Yahweh]." In other words, these verses declare that Ezekiel would spend the seven and one-half years until the fall of Jerusalem (cf. 33:22) withdrawn from the community of the exiles and muted by God except to announce the warnings of God's judgments, which God would enable him to recite, to those who came to him. Israel initially rejected

THE BIBLE

This book contains the mind of God, the state of man, the way of salvation, the doom of sinners, and the happiness of believers. Its doctrine is holy, its precepts are binding, its histories are true, and its decisions are immutable. Read it to be wise, believe it to be safe, and practice it to be holy.

It contains light to direct you, food to support you, and comfort to cheer you. It is the traveller's map, the pilgrim's staff, the pilot's compass, the soldier's sword, and the Christian's charter.

Here, heaven is opened and the gates of hell disclosed. **Christ is its grand subject,** our good its design, and the glory of God its end. It should fill the memory, rule the heart, and guide the feet.

Read it slowly, frequently, prayerfully. It is a mine of wealth, a paradise of glory, and a river of pleasure. It is given you in life, will be opened at the judgment, and will be remembered forever. It involves the highest responsibility, will reward faithful labor, and will condemn all who trifle with its sacred contents.

'Tis the Book that has for ages

Lifted man from sin and shame.
That great message on its pages
Will **forever** be the same.

Never compare the Bible with other books. Comparisons are dangerous. Books speak from earth; the Bible speaks from heaven. Never think or say that the Bible contains the Word of God; it IS the Word of God. It is supernatural in origin, eternal in duration, inexpressible in value, infinite in scope, divine in authorship, regenerative in power, infallible in authority, universal in interest, personal in application, **inspired in totality**. Read it through. Write it down. Pray it in. Work it out. Pass it on. **It is the Word of God.**

—Selected

"All scripture is given by the inspiration of God, and is profitable for doctrine, for reproof, for correction, for instruction in righteousness: That the man of God may be perfect, thoroughly furnished unto all good works" (II Timothy 3:16-17).

"For ever, O Lord, thy word is settled in heaven" (Psalm 119:89).

"Thy word have I hid in mine heart, that I might not sin against thee" (Psalm 119:11).

Osterhus Pub. House, 4500 W. Broadway, Minneapolis, MN 55422
This tract costs $1 for 100; $2.50 for 500; $4 for 1000
Postage: add 30 percent (not only 30¢)

him, but later the elders of Israel sneaked away to the prophet to inquire of God's workings. Thus he would not be a direct reprover to the whole nation.

ENCOURAGEMENT AND PREPARATION

It is God who always sends forth His spokesmen (2:3). When Ezekiel fell prostrate before the Almighty God, or when he had to stand before men, it was the Spirit of God who enabled him, and the hand of Yahweh which strengthened and consoled him when the anguish of his task became too great (1:3; 2:4; 3:12-14, 22-23). God never sends forth His servant without the necessary equipment for the mission. God told Ezekiel that He would give him a hard head and face, harder than that of rebellious Israel, to enable him to stand against her obstinance and stubbornness (3:8-9). As a result, there would be no need for Ezekiel to fear the people or their words, though they would continue to prick him and sting him like scorpions (2:6). Neither would he need to be dismayed and give up when he stood before them and they rebelled (2:6). "God will strengthen" Ezekiel (the meaning of his name).

2

THE DISOBEDIENCE OF JUDAH AND HER PREDICTED JUDGMENT

4:1—24:27

THE WATCHMAN'S INITIAL WARNING OF JUDGMENT
(4:1—7:27)

SUMMARY

As a priest, Ezekiel had to know the Mosaic covenant, to uphold it, and to constantly apply it to the situations facing the nation of Israel and her inhabitants. This is exactly what Ezekiel did in his first message of warning. In order to understand this portion of the prophecy as well as the entire book, read the Mosaic covenant (Ex 20 through Deu), especially Leviticus 26 and Deuteronomy 28-32, which outline the blessings which would come upon Israel if they kept the covenant, and the judgments which would come if they failed to walk in God's ways as outlined in that covenant. As you study the first twenty-four chapters of Ezekiel you will continually hear the words of Leviticus and Deuteronomy ringing in your ears.

Ezekiel's first warning to Israel was symbolically portrayed, then orally announced. He did not speak to an audience, though people undoubtedly saw and heard this message from God as he performed it. It was like watching a play.

The stage props were first introduced. Ezekiel was to etch a picture of the city of Jerusalem on a clay brick tile. He then inscribed the war equipment of a siege around the city (4:1-3). Next Ezekiel came "on stage" to depict the siege by lying first on one of his sides and then on the other for 430 days and placing an iron plate between himself and the inscribed city as a demonstration of the severity of the siege that would come upon Jerusalem (4:4-8). This drama was a sign to Judah that she would have to bear the burden of her iniquity through the coming siege and exile (4:3). The severity of this siege was heightened by the rationed food that Ezekiel ate as he depicted the siege (4:9-17). He would mix foods that one does not normally combine in order to get sufficient meal to bake cakes. He would be forced to eat this food by weight and measure so that it had to be rationed properly. Being a priest, he complained against eating defiled food cooked over human dung, so the Lord graciously let him heat the cooking stones over cow's dung (4:14-17).

What would happen after the seige? Exile! Chapter 5 presents scene two of the act (5:1-4, 12). Ezekiel took a razor and cut his hair. Weighing it on a balance in order to divide it into three equal parts, he then burned one-third of it by fire on the inscribed city of Jerusalem as he lay there. A second third he struck with a sword as it was placed around the inscribed city. The last third was scattered to the wind. Of that last third, Ezekiel was to keep a few hairs tucked inside the hem of his garment for safety. The rest would be burned or struck with the sword.

What had all this acting portrayed? The Lord interpreted it for those who might not understand initially (5:5-17). The city was Jerusalem, a city which was central among the nations in the outworking of God's program (cf. Ps 132:13-18). This city and the nation of Israel, because of their abominable and idolatrous iniquity over the years, would finally be judged by the Lord through the Babylonians (cf. 2 Ki 25), as Moses declared in Levitcus 26 and Deuteronomy 32. A siege would be the means of judgment upon the city. When the siege occurred, famine would strike the city to the extent that parents would eat their children and vice versa (cf. Lev 26:29; Deu 28:53; Lam 4:10). The children of Israel would eat defiled food during the siege and in the lands of exile (Eze 4:13). One-third of the inhabitants of Jerusalem would die in fire, pestilence, and famine within the city during the siege (2 Ki 25:3, 9). A second third would be slain by the sword in the environs around Jerusalem as they sought to escape (cf. 2 Ki 25:18-21a; 2 Ch 36:17). The last third would be scattered to the wind in exile (2 Ki 25:11, 21b). Of those exiles, some would be burned and others slain by the sword in foreign lands. Only a small number of the exiles would be tucked securely into the hem of God's garment as a safe remnant. Yahweh would not have pity on Jerusalem to spare it as He had in the past. His justice would be exercised in keeping the covenant (Lev 26). When the judgment was complete, the people would know that Yahweh had spoken and acted.

But Jerusalem was not the only guilty member among Israel. As the capital, she represented the entire nation. Lest anyone think that the rest of the land was innocent, the Lord commanded Ezekiel in chapters 6 and 7 to turn and face the mountains of Israel and announce a prophecy against the entire land. The invaders would purge the entire land of its idolatry by destroying all the places of pagan worship. A remnant would be spared and mourn during their exile over the iniquity that they had brought upon the land of Israel (6:1-10). With great exclamation of lament, Ezekiel bemoaned the fact that no one would remain untouched by the judgment of God (6:3). The Lord wanted all Judah to know that He is Yahweh (6:7). They had obviously forgotten their covenant God in the midst of their prolonged idolatry (6:11-14).

This judgment of God was imminent (7:1-18). It would be a time of panic. Everyone would be caught right where he was—inside or outside the city—unable to complete business deals or to go forth to battle. Yahweh is the Judge. He would judge them according to their ways (not words), placing their abominations upon them and punishing them as they would punish others (7:3, 8, 9, 27). All would be affected. Only a few would escape, and, in their weakened condition, they would mourn their iniquity (7:16-18).

No help would be available to anyone when God's judgment came. Silver and gold would buy neither food nor deliverance. Wealth had been Judah's stumbling block, and now it would be given as spoil to the invaders. No leaders would offer any help at this time. The prophets would have no vision when one was sought. The priests would have no counsel or comfort from the Law, since it was being fulfilled. The kings and princes would be mourning. Everyone must stand alone before the great God who judges iniquity. No man or material could help at this time (7:19-27). Why would this happen? In order that Israel would know that the Lord is Yahweh their God (cf. 7:4, 9, 27).

THE IRON PLATE (PAN) (4:3)

As Ezekiel acted out the siege of the city, the significance of placing the iron pan or plate between him and the inscribed city has puzzled many an expositor. The author does not claim to be an exception. Some have thought that the pan represents the severity of the siege against the city, while others view it as a symbol of the barrier of sin that Israel had erected between herself and God. There appears to be no import to the use of the pan, since that term is only used in the Old Testament to indicate the specific type of pan employed by the priests in baking the cereal offerings (Lev 2:5; 6:21; 7:9). Ezekiel, being a priest, would probably have had such a pan. Whether "iron" has significance is unknown. It is clear that Ezekiel was to face the city with the pan as a "wall" between him and the city, and lay siege to the city. Normally a wall is for protection. Ezekiel had been promised protection against those who would seek to "prick" him when they heard his message. The same was true of Jeremiah (Jer 1:18), whom God made an "iron pillar" to withstand Israel's rebellion. Perhaps, then, what is meant to be conveyed by this symbol is that Ezekiel would be protected as he pronounced judgment upon Jerusalem.

THE DAYS OF LYING ON THE LEFT AND RIGHT SIDES (4:4-8)

The confusion that has arisen in seeking to make sense of 390 and forty days has led to innumerable guesses as to the interpretation of these numbers as well as alterations of the text. Altering the text is not the way to solve the problem, for there is really no textual reason not to accept these numbers as they are. The passage makes it very clear that each day Ezekiel lay on his side represented a year during which the nation would bear the burden of judgment for her past iniquity (cf. Num 14:34). All numbering in the book of Ezekiel is rendered according to the captivity of Jehoiachin (597 B.C.) and therefore should be calculated forward and not backward, as many have done. Numbering back in the history of Israel produces only chaos, for 390 years prior to the deportation in 597 B.C. would produce the date of 987 B.C., which has no significance historically, and an additional forty years would add up to 1027 B.C., which likewise has no meaning.

Another factor must be considered. The 390 years is a separate and distinct number for the Northern Kingdom of Israel, whereas the forty years is for the iniquity of the Southern Kingdom, Judah. The 390 years does not include the forty years according to the reading of 4:5-6. Some have advocated the inclusion of the forty years into the 390 years on the basis of verse 9, but that verse does not seem to warrant such an inclusion. Verse 9 only tells how long Ezekiel was to eat defiled bread. Therefore, the combined total is 430 years (390 for the bearing of Israel's iniquity and 40 for the bearing of the iniquity of Judah). These 430 years should follow the captivity of Jehoiachin (597 B.C.) to show the number of years that the nations would be in subjection to the foreign powers. This would give us a concluding date of approximately 167 B.C., the year that the Maccabean revolt began and the Jews once again exercised rule over the land of Canaan for the first time since 597 B.C.

DEFILED FOOD (4:9-17)

Leviticus 26:14-29 speaks of the hunger that would exist during the future punishment and siege of the people of Israel. Mixing grains was not really contrary to the Mosaic covenant, though eating defiled food was wrong (cf. Lev 22:8; Deu 12:16; 14:21; 23:12-14; Eze 44:31). Cooking over human dung disturbed Ezekiel, and the Lord graciously changed that. The significance of defiled bread was important, however, for the passage goes on to declare that they would eat the bread of foreigners, which would not be kosher, and therefore they would be defiled (cf. Dan 1:1-18). The central point of this portion is to make clear that there would be famine in the land at the time of God's judgment, as Leviticus 26:26 declares. The "staff of bread" (4:16) would be shattered; "they will be appalled with one another" (v. 17, NASB; cf. Lev 26:16); and they would "pine away in their iniquity" (4:17, ASV; cf. Lev 26:16, 39). Those who would manage to escape death would be as exiles and still would eat the defiled bread of foreigners.

SHAVING THE HEAD AND FACE (5:1-4)

Shaving the head and beard in the ancient Near East was a sign of disgrace and humiliation (cf. 2 Sa 10:4; Eze 7:18), and it also was a symbol of mourning (cf. Is 22:12; Eze 27:31; Jer 16:6; Amos 8:10).

Leviticus 21:5 says that a priest was defiled if he shaved and was no longer holy to Yahweh. Deuteronomy 14:1 exhorts Israel not to be bald in mourning for the dead, since that was a heathen practice of the land. The significance of Ezekiel's shaving, therefore, seems to be that he was depicting mourning for the nation which was defiled and no longer holy before the Lord. Judah has become like the pagan nations in their idolatrous worship: disgraceful and humiliating.

THE DIVISION OF THE HAIR (5:1-4, 12)

The first third of the hair described in verse 2 was to be burned. Verse 12 adds that members of this group also would die from the pestilence or waste away in famine. The statements of verses 3 and 4 may present some confusion. In verse 3 the place from which the "few" are taken is described as "there" in the Hebrew text. The near antecedent is the "third" that was scattered to the wind. These "few" that were placed in security in the hem of Ezekiel's garment were a remnant from those scattered in exile. Verse 4 then declares that Ezekiel was to take from them again (i.e., the same group of the scattered exiles) and cast some into the midst of the fire. Evidently the fire of judgment took the lives of some of the exiles.

THE RELATION OF THIS MESSAGE TO THE MOSAIC COVENANT

In 5:5-7 the reason for this judgment is explained. Israel had rebelled against God's judgments and refused to walk in His statutes. As a result she had become more wicked than other nations. "Judgments" and "statutes" refer to those principles set forth in the Mosaic covenant (cf. Ex 24:3; Lev 19; Deu 4-5; Eze 20:11). In this Law code the nation was warned not to walk in the statutes of the other nations (Lev 18:3-5). She would be judged if she failed to keep the statutes of God's covenant (cf. Lev 26:3, 15; Deu 8:11-20; 28; 30:11-20). By Ezekiel's time, however, the people of Israel had, or would have had at the destruction of Jerusalem, broken the Mosaic covenant by eating members of their own families (cf. Lev 26:29; Deu 28:53), and defiled the sanctuary with idolatry (cf. Ex 20:3-7; Lev 19:30; 20:3; 21:22-23; 26:2; 2 Ki 21:2-11; 2 Ch 36:8; Jer 7:8-11). Judgment would be meted out in accordance with the stipulations of the Mosaic covenant (cf. Deu 29-30).

Israel would become a reproach and taunt to other nations (Eze 5:14-15; cf. Lev 26:31-33; Deu 29:23-28). Evil arrows (Eze 5:16; cf. Deu 32:23) as well as evil animals (Eze 5:17; cf. Deu 32:24) would be sent against her for destruction. In the midst of judgment she would prepare to go forth in battle but would not succeed (Eze 7:14; cf. Lev 26:17). Israel would become so lawless that she would not only refuse to keep God's laws, but she would even fail to walk in the legal stipulations of other *pagan* nations.

REMNANT (5:3; 6:8-9; 7:16-18)

In addition to the implied reference to a remnant in 5:3, there is the explicit statement in 6:8-9 that a remnant would escape and be scattered among the nations. This remnant would be reminded of how they committed spiritual adultery by going after idols and thereby having affairs with other gods. They would then mourn their iniquity (cf. 7:16-18).

UNIQUENESS OF THIS JUDGMENT (5:8-9)

In 5:8-9 it is stated that Yahweh has never executed judgment like this before and will never mete out judgment like it again. This does not mean, however, that a different and more severe judgment could not occur in the future, like that mentioned in Joel 2:2. The context is the determining factor in deciding which judgment is meant and its finality. The context of chapter 5 is concerned about the unique forthcoming destruction of Jerusalem in 586 B.C.

WHY JUDGMENT UPON THE MOUNTAINS OF ISRAEL (6:1-14)?

Chapter 6 begins with Yahweh calling upon Ezekiel to prophesy against the mountains, hills, valleys, and stream beds of Israel. This seems somewhat strange until one realizes that Canaanite religion employed the hilltops and valleys for their major places of idolatrous worship. This passage indicates that Judah was practicing Canaanite religion when God stated that He would destroy the high places, sun pillars, and altars (6:3-6; cf. Lev 26:30). The reason for eliminating these objects of false worship was to demonstrate that they were nothing and, on the other hand, that the Lord alone is Yahweh. "And ye shall know that I

26

am the LORD [Yahweh]" is a phrase repeated at least sixty-eight times throughout this book. This emphasis shows that the Lord was seeking to instruct Israel through this judgment that He, and He alone, is to be worshiped, just as He instructed Israel initially in the first three commandments of the Decalogue (Ex 20:3-7). Canaanite religion, with its emphasis upon polytheism, bloodshed, perverted sexual ritual, child sacrifice and snake worship, was a constant plague to the people of Israel throughout their history. Canaanite religion was syncretistic, assimilating any and every thing. Israel kept finding herself enticed to join the Canaanites. God continually warned His people against this practice (Num 33:50-56; Deu 18:10-12; 20:16-18) and predicted ultimate judgment upon them if they pursued idolatrous Canaanite ritual (Deu 29:16-28; 30:15-20). Ezekiel was picking up this theme as a reminder to Israel as to why judgment was now coming.

CLAPPING THE HANDS (6:11)

Clapping was either a sign of joyous praise or one of derision over sin and judgment (cf. Lam 2:15; Eze 21:14-17; 22:13; 25:6; Nah 3:19). Clapping his hands and stomping his feet were commanded of Ezekiel to demonstrate the remorse and derision he was to show toward Israel because of her sin and the coming judgment.

MANNER OF JUDGMENT (7:3, 8-9, 27)

The people of Israel were to be judged according to their ways. They would be judged by what they did and how they lived, not just by what they said. They would be held responsible for their abominable practices, and be examined according to their own judgments, that is, those written in their constitution, the Mosaic covenant (cf. Lev 26; Deu 28-30).

A BUDDING ROD (7:10)

The "rod" is often employed as a symbol of the dominion of the Israelite kings (cf. Ps 2; 110). Ezekiel appears to be saying that the Lord was coming to judge Israel whose kings and rulers have "budded" and "blossomed" with insolence and violence in their reigns, rather than follow the way that Yahweh had directed. Thus they would be judged by the true King, Yahweh (cf. 2 Sa 7:14).

THE BUYER AND SELLER (7:12-13)

The context of the statements about buying and selling is the imminency, permanency and completeness of the judgment and exile. According to the Mosaic covenant, when a man sold his land in order to pay a debt, that land was to be restored to him in the sabbatical year or the year of jubilee. However, Ezekiel declared that the captivity would make it impossible for such a man to return to his property in the sabbatical or jubilee year, since he would not be in the land. It is clearly shown that the permanency of the exile for that generation was sure; the seller would not ever see his land again. This affects all the inhabitants of Israel, for verse 13 states that this vision of judgment upon all the multitude would not be turned back. It is certain.

SILVER AND GOLD (7:19-22)

The Lord made it very clear that money would not suffice during the time of siege and famine. It would neither buy food nor deliverance. In fact, gold and silver had been Judah's stumbling block through pride of possession and their usage to create idols. God will give them to the foreign invaders for spoil. They shall take them and the treasures of God and profane them. These treasures must refer to the Temple treasures which were taken into captivity by Nebuchadnezzar (cf. 2 Ki 25:13-17; 2 Ch 36:18).

MAKE A CHAIN (7:23)

The symbolism involved in this command to Ezekiel undoubtedly refers to binding Israel, as captives were bound, so that she might go into exile to Babylon in discipline for her iniquity.

SEEKING HELP (7:25-27)

There would be no help from men in the time of judgment. At that time Israel finally would desire to hear the visions and messages of the prophets. Her ears would listen attentively to the Law from the priests and to the counsel of the elders. The only problem is that there would be no visions, no words from priests and no counsel from the elders. It was too late! God's judgment had come.

THE DEPARTURE OF THE GLORY OF YAHWEH FROM JERUSALEM
(8:1—11:25)

SUMMARY

In his first vision and message Ezekiel announced that the Almighty God of glory would execute judgment upon Jerusalem and the land of Israel because of the failure of the people of Judah to obey the covenant which God gave to Moses. Then Ezekiel, by lying 430 days on his two sides, acted out the siege which would come upon the city. One year and two months had passed (cf. 1:1-3 and 8:1) and now Ezekiel was fulfilling the picture lesson of forty days on his side for the iniquity of Judah. The elders of exiled Hebrews had come to sit and learn from Ezekiel, who already had had a unique ministry of warning Israel through symbolic actions. They were probably watching his every movement in order to understand its meaning. Once again, on about the 413th day, Ezekiel was suddenly enveloped by visions of the God of glory.

It is not by chance that this vision occurred during the time in which Ezekiel was lying on his right side depicting the judgment for Judah's iniquity. At this time only Judah was left in the land of Canaan, and the forthcoming vision would concern Judah's capital city, Jerusalem. In Jerusalem, the situation had been increasingly deteriorating politically and religiously since Ezekiel had begun his symbolic ministry. Jerusalem, the city chosen by God for His habitation (cf. 2 Sa 7; Ps 132), was the central sanctuary of Israel, her unifying center where the tribal units were to express their obedience and loyalty to Yahweh. But in Ezekiel's day this city center had become the rotten core of Israel's apostasy. The corruption of the leaders and the sanctuary itself (cf. 9:6) had to be exposed and judged as the major problem of the nation. Therefore, while Ezekiel was acting out his siege of Jerusalem, God again appeared to him in a vision to indict Jerusalem, His holy habitation among His people.

The vision follows the same form outlined in Ezekiel 1. The date is given first: August-September, 592 B.C. The recipient of the vision is Ezekiel, and the setting in which Ezekiel received this vision involved the elders of Judah (in exile) sitting before him while he was lying on his right side in keeping with the command of 4:6 (cf. 8:1). Ezekiel then was transported in the vision to Jerusalem by the Spirit and by the hand of the Lord, the God of glory whom he had seen in the first vision (8:2-3a).

In Jerusalem, Ezekiel was shown the great abominations of the house of Israel (Eze 8). At the north gate of the inner court he saw a statue which provoked Yahweh to jealous anger: the seemingly well-known "image of jealousy." Perhaps this was the image of the Canaanite goddess Asherah which Manasseh, the king of Judah, had placed in the sanctuary; later it was removed (cf. 2 Ch 33:7, 15), and then it was reestablished after Josiah's reform. Even if it was not of Asherah, it most certainly was a well-known idol which was standing in the northern outer courtyard of the Temple, which was a grave abomination to the Lord (Eze 8:3-6).

The Lord then directed Ezekiel to dig a hole into the north wall surrounding the inner court. There he observed seventy elders of Judah, leaders of the nation who were selected according to a pattern developed under Moses. Originally the elders were to aid Moses in upholding the Mosaic covenant and in guiding the people. They were being led by Jaazaniah, son of Shaphan, who was burning incense in worship to carvings of every sort of creeping thing and detestable animal (cf. Lev 11). These leaders of the nation had become perverted in secret idolatry. Why? Because they felt that God had abandoned the nation, allowing the deportations of Judah in 605 and 597 B.C. Therefore, they, in turn, had abandoned God, assuming that He did not exist since He had not protected them. These leaders, who thought that God could not see what they were doing, had given up any idea of turning back to Yahweh, and now they were even denying His existence. Thus the leadership of the nation did not know Yahweh, their unchanging and faithful God, nor did they understand His covenant with Moses (Eze 8:7-13).

But there were more abominations for Ezekiel to witness. God took him to the north gate of the Temple where women were seated, weeping for Tammuz, the ancient Babylonian god of vegetation and floods. This old fertility rite was common throughout the ages in the Near East. Now the women of Israel had adopted its practice. Since the vision took place in August, the hot and dry time of the year, these women undoubtedly were weeping for Tammuz to be revived and the fertility of the land to be restored. They had forgotten that it was Yahweh alone who could bring the rains upon the land and make the land productive (8:14-15; cf. Ps 29; 93).

Finally Ezekiel was brought into the inner court, the area restricted to the priests (cf. 2 Ch 4:9; Joel 2:17). Certainly one would expect the priests to maintain the Law and the worship of Yahweh. Yet Ezekiel saw twenty-five of them facing east, worshiping Shamash, the sun-god of the Babylonians. Even these religious leaders had turned from God. In repudiation they were turning their backs on the Temple (cf. 2 Ch 29:6) and breaking the Mosaic covenant by their idolatrous actions (8:16-17; cf. Deu 4:19).

Having so easily turned from Yahweh, the people of Judah filled the land with violence. The political and religious leadership of the nation was thoroughly corrupt. Having provoked Yahweh to wrath, He would judge them without compassion, though they shouted to Him. The people had deliberately defied Yahweh and broken His covenant (8:17-18).

The judgment announced in 8:18 is immediately symbolized in the visions of chapters 9 and 10. Exiting through the upper north gate (2 Ki 15:35; 2 Ch 27:3) were six officials, each with an instrument of destruction in his hand. A seventh individual among them was dressed in white linen, carrying a scribe's inkhorn.

At this point Ezekiel saw the manifestation of God's glory rising from the cherub in the Holy of Holies and moving to the threshold of the Temple. This glorious God of judgment was about to execute His judgment upon these idolatrous worshipers who had defiled the Temple precinct. The departure of the glory of God from the Temple, Jerusalem, and Judah is a significant theme in Ezekiel's prophecy. God would not be simply another god in a pantheon worshiped by the leaders of Israel. He is God alone, and Israel is to worship none other but Him (Ex 20:1-7). Therefore, He was departing from Israel as He had warned in Deuteronomy 31:17 and Hosea 9:12. He would leave the nation temporarily as it underwent discipline. But one day the glory of God will return to Jerusalem when God restores His people to their land, according to Ezekiel 43.

As the glory of God stood over the threshold of the Temple, God commanded protection for those who repented of their iniquity, and judgment upon those who did not. The man with the inkhorn went forth and marked the foreheads of all those who mourned over the abominations which were done in Jerusalem (cf. Rev 7:3; 9:4; 14:1). This was a mark of protection from the judgment to come. The other six men in the vision were sent to smite the unrepentant people, beginning in the sanctuary with the idolatrous leaders. They were to have no compassion on these leaders, for they were the heart of Judah's problem. However, the six officials were exhorted not to approach any with the ink mark on their foreheads. Even as the leaders had defiled the sanctuary with their abominations, so it would be further defiled with the dead (Num 19:11; 2 Ki 23:16) in its courts (Eze 9:1-7).

Though God promised a remnant (Eze 6:8), Ezekiel feared that the remnant in exile would now be destroyed, and he requested their protection. God temporarily ignored Ezekiel's request to emphasize again the reason for the judgment. God wanted the issue to be clear: the judgment was coming upon the house of Judah because their iniquity was *very* great. The people had turned from God, ignoring His existence, believing that He had forsaken the land forever. This demanded judgment! If one was in exile and had been spared by being there, then that one was not the present issue. Ezekiel and all others must not miss the import of the judgment and its reason. God would not have compassion but would put the judgment of the ways of these people on their own heads. They were responsible and had to bear the consequences of their deeds (9:8-11).

Then Ezekiel watched the glory of God at the threshold of the Temple. This was the same manifestation of God's glory as was discussed in detail in chapter 1 (cf. 10:15, 19, 20, 22). The man with the inkhorn returned from giving the mark of protection to the righteous, and was sent forth again with the fire of God's judgment. He took coals from the fire which was in the midst of the cherubim—the purifying fire of God's judgment—and poured them out on Jerusalem. When this was accomplished, the glory of God moved to the east gate of the Temple (10:1-22).

As God's glory moved to the Temple's east gate, the Spirit brought Ezekiel there also. From this gate Ezekiel viewed one final manifestation of the corruption of Jerusalem's leaders. Twenty-five men stood in the gate under the leadership of two princes of the people. These were unquestionably political leaders of some sort who are described as those who were devising iniquity and giving counsel to the city. What was their counsel? It was that those in exile should not build houses and settle down, as Jeremiah had urged them to do (Jer 29:5), because they claimed the captivity would not be as long as Jeremiah had implied. Likewise, they argued that the inhabitants of Jerusalem were secure in Jerusalem just as meat is secure from the burning of fire while it is in a pot. The exile would soon be over; ignore the prophets' judgment, they advised (11:1-3).

During the vision the Spirit prophesied through Ezekiel concerning these political leaders. "Tell them, Ezekiel, that their ways and thoughts are not hid from Me, for I know what is in their spirit. I know they have murdered and committed violence. Therefore, the pot of Jerusalem will become the pot of judgment, not protection. Security will not be found within her; rather, the leaders will be taken out of the pot of Jerusalem and slain by the sword of strangers on the borders of Israel" (cf. 2 Ki 25:18-21). Why was Yahweh doing this? So that Israel might know that He is Yahweh (Eze 11:10, 12). God had threatened cursing for disobedience to the Mosaic covenant, and He is a faithful God who was now executing that judgment. What had Israel done to deserve this wrath? She had followed the way of life of the nations around her, as manifested by the abominations within the Temple area observed in this section, rather than following and doing God's ways as revealed in her constitution, the Mosaic covenant. The issue was not one of just knowing these statutes, but of doing them (Lev 18:3-5). When Ezekiel had finished this brief prophecy, Pelatiah ben Benaiah, one of the two leaders, dropped dead, giving an immediate demonstration of the severity of God's judgment (Eze 11:4-13).

Ezekiel remained extremely concerned about the fate of the remnant. Yahweh replied that He would be a sanctuary to them. He would be ever present, making provisions for His own no matter where they were. In addition Yahweh recalled the promise of restoration after judgment (Deu 30). He would regather Israel from among the nations, cleanse the land of Canaan from the abominations, and restore His people to their land. There Yahweh would institute the new covenant

33

(cf. Jer 31:31-40; Eze 36:26-27; Deu 30:6) with Israel by removing her obstinate heart of stone and replacing it with a new spirit and a willing, devoted heart. Yahweh would do this to enable Israel to walk in His ways. Then Israel would be as God always meant her to be, His people rather than just another nation, and He would be her God. Yet Yahweh reminded Ezekiel that all whose hearts followed after the idolatrous abominations would bear the judgment for their ways (Eze 11:13-21).

With this final message of hope for the remnant, the glory of God departed from the Temple area to the Mount of Olives on the east in a final show of departure from Jerusalem and Judah as the judgment then went forth. Then in the vision Ezekiel returned to his house in Babylon, and the vision left him. He then recounted the vision to the exiles (Eze 11:22-25).

IDOLATROUS ABOMINATIONS (8:1-18)

Various idolatrous rituals were being practiced by the leaders in Jerusalem. The worship of *carved detestable animals and creeping things (8:10-12)* was similar to the animalistic motifs worshiped both in Egypt and Mesopotamia. But perhaps it was not an adoption of a foreign religious act at all, but rather the outright defiance of the Mosaic code (Lev 11) by the elders of Israel.

The image of jealousy (8:5). This was a statue which provoked Yahweh to anger by its prominence in the outer court and its idolatrous character. This statue might have been the reestablished image of jealousy, Asherah, placed in the sanctuary originally by Manasseh and later removed by him, but that is only conjecture. The exact identity is unknown, yet it illustrates the blatant idolatry of the people of Israel.

Tammuz worship (8:14). This worship was well known. This Akkadian god of vegetation and fertility was another of the many manifestations of the fertility gods. The people thought that, like Baal and Hadad, Tammuz brought rain to the earth and the refreshment of lush vegetation in the spring. In the dry periods of the year he would "die," only to be revived by the wailing of Ishtar. Apparently in Ezekiel's vision the women were trying to "revive" Tammuz in that month of August.

They believed that the bursting blossoms of spring would mark his revival and his return in response to their weeping.

Sun worship (8:16). This was also an old religion, forbidden in the Mosaic code (Deu 4:19). Josiah had removed this ritual from Judah in his reformation (2 Ki 23:5, 11). But once again it had been revived, this time by the priests. These twenty-five men were probably priests, since the Scripture indicates that only priests were permitted into the inner court of the Temple (cf. 2 Ch 4:9; Joel 2:17). They had transferred their service to the sun-god (Shamash of the Babylonians, most likely) and turned their backs on their true Temple service (cf. 2 Ch 29:6-7).

The phrase *"twig to their nose"* (8:17, NASB) is perplexing. Many conjectures as to its meaning have been set forth. Saggs has recently supported the thesis that this was part of the ritual form and gesture in the Mesopotamian worship of the sun-god.[1] Perhaps he is right. Regardless of the correctness of his view, the context implies that it was some form of idolatrous ritual which was extremely offensive to Yahweh.

This idolatrous worship by the Jerusalem leaders is a major emphasis in this vision. God wanted the people of Israel to know clearly why judgment was coming. They had "exchanged the glory of the incorruptible God for an image in the form of corruptible man and of birds and four-footed animals and crawling creatures . . . and worshiped and served the creature rather than the Creator" (Ro 1:23-25, NASB). They had broken the first three commandments of the Decalogue (Ex 20:3-7), both by their words and their actions.

REASONS FOR JUDGMENT

The previous paragraph led into the discussion of the causes for God's wrath. Several times throughout these four chapters those reasons were made clear. First and foremost, the people had committed idolatry, as demonstrated above. The emphasis was upon their *doing* of these abominable rituals (Eze 8:6, 9, 13, 17). In addition, they had filled the land with violence (8:17), filling the streets of Jerusalem with perver-

1. H. W. F. Saggs, "Notes and Studies: The Branch to the Nose," *The Journal of Theological Studies* 11 (October 1960): 318-29.

sion and bloodshed (9:9; 11:6). The leaders had denied the faithfulness of Yahweh to His covenant with Abraham, feeling that He had forsaken their land. They also denied His omniscience (8:12; 9:9). All of this is summed up in 11:12 when the Lord declared that Israel had failed to walk in His statutes and precepts as set forth in the Mosaic covenant. Rather, Israel had sought to follow the precepts of the nations around her. When Israel turned from God's ways of living to man's way of life, the resulting threat of Yahweh was that she would be disciplined in order that she *might know that He is Yahweh* (Lev 18:3-30). The whole purpose of God's judgment upon Israel was to cause her to know that He really *is* Yahweh and that the best way to live is according to the precepts revealed in the Mosaic covenant.

IDENTITY OF THE SEVEN MEN OF CHAPTER NINE

Six men appeared in chapter 9 with instruments of destruction in their hands. A seventh among them was clothed in white linen and carried a scribe's inkhorn. No specific identity is given of any of the seven. They were probably angelic creatures administering God's judgment and protection. White linen was worn by priests and normally symbolized God's holiness, which is certainly involved in His protection and judgment. One should not seek to make much out of the number seven, though many have tried.

THE MARK OF THE MAN WITH THE INKHORN (9:4)

The Hebrew term for "mark" was initially formed by a crossing of two lines similar to our plus sign (+). This may have been the "mark" that was placed upon the foreheads of the righteous in this passage. Many have sought to find symbolism in the mark, such as a prefiguring of the cross. That Ezekiel, or even the Lord, had this in mind is only conjecture. The type of mark is not really significant. The important factor is that God marked those who righteously mourned over the abominations of Jerusalem, and they would be delivered from the coming judgment of the other six men. Similar markings of the righteous by God are found elsewhere in Scripture (cf. Ex 12; Rev 7:3; 9:4; 14:1).

IDENTITY OF THE CHERUBIM (10:1-22)

Ezekiel identified the "living beings" of the vision in chapter 1 as "cherubim" (10:14-15, 18-20, 22). Perhaps this was because Ezekiel had a closer look at them in the inner court and could relate them to the cherubim of the Temple decor. The fact that one of the cherubs is described as having the face of an "ox" in chapter 1 and the face of a "cherub" in chapter 10 has created much consternation. There are two possible solutions. Either (1) Ezekiel was seeing primarily the one side of the whole cherubim throne of God's glory and referred to it as the face of a cherub in chapter 10, or (2) the ox was the normal understanding of the face of a cherub. Cherubim in the ancient Near East, as well as in the Old Testament, were frequently considered to be angelic beings with the basic form of an animal, the head of a man (but with differing faces), and wings.

The coals of fire from which the hands of the cherubim gathered the coals to give to the man with the inkhorn to scatter over Jerusalem were located in the midst of the four cherubim. Taken in context, these coals represented the fire of judgment which God was pouring out upon the city.

ICHABOD

The name of Ichabod was given to the child born to Eli's daughter-in-law in 1 Samuel 4 when it was learned that her husband was dead, the Ark was stolen, the high priest Eli was dead, and the army defeated. The woman died in childbirth, naming her son Ichabod, meaning "the glory has departed." That name equally applies to these chapters. The glory of God left its residence in the Temple, going from the Holy of Holies to the threshold of the Temple (8:3), then to the east gate (10:19), and finally to the Mount of Olives east of the city (11:23). God's glory left the polluted city with its idolatrous abominations as the judgments upon her began.

THE REMNANT (9:4, 8; 11:13-21)

Ezekiel already had been instructed about the remnant in chapter 6. This caused him to cry out twice to God concerning the safety of the remnant during judgment. God made several things clear: (1) The righteous who mourned the iniquities of the city of Jerusalem would receive a mark on their foreheads and thereby not be touched by the destruction (9:4). (2) They would be rejected and sent away by their brethren (11:15). (3) Yahweh would be a sanctuary of refuge to them, though He would scatter them among the nations (11:16). (4) Yahweh would regather them, restore them to the land of Canaan as promised in Deuteronomy 30, cleanse the land of its idolatry, give them a single heart of flesh in place of the obstinate heart of stone, and give them a new spirit (Eze 11:17-19). (5) The purpose of all this was to enable the remnant to return and follow God's covenant ways in their land so that He would be their God and they would truly be His people (11:20). This is the first mention of restoration in the book of Ezekiel.

TWENTY-FIVE MEN (8:16; 11:1)

Were these two groups of twenty-five men the same or different? We cannot really know. The similarity of numbers does not mean the identity of the groups. The first group was certainly priests, as discussed above. The latter group included two princes of the people, but that would not preclude that group from also being the group of priests.

ANSWERS TO THE EXILES' FALSE OPTIMISM (12:1—19:14)

SUMMARY

Since this section is longer than those discussed previously, the procedure will vary slightly. An overall argument of this entire section is set forth. Then the individual portions within this section are discussed and analyzed separately.

This section of Ezekiel's prophecy does not begin with a chronological notice, but its close proximity to the preceding vision and its unique relationship to it would tend to argue for Ezekiel's deliverance of the messages in this section shortly after the declaration of the previous vision in chapters 8-11. The book has followed a basic pattern thus far: each vision is followed by a message, or series of messages, which develops the meaning of the preceding vision and treats the problems and questions which may have arisen in the minds of Ezekiel's hearers. Just as chapters 4-7 elaborated the judgments of the glorious God seen in the initial vision of chapters 1-3, so these messages of chapters 12-19 were primarily delivered to challenge the persistent optimism of the exiles who believed that the judgments announced in the vision of chapters 8-11 were not really going to occur.

Ezekiel's task here was to reinforce the announcement of Jerusalem's coming judgment by refuting the erroneous bases of the exiles' confidence which led them to believe that the kingdom of Judah and its capital, Jerusalem, would still be preserved. The section begins with God reminding Ezekiel that he was speaking to the rebellious house (12:1-2; cf. 2:3-8), which, though having ears and eyes, had yet to hear and see the prophetic message, even the recent messages of Ezekiel. Instead, the Israelite exiles were still hoping for an early return to the land of Canaan and for the preservation of Jerusalem and Judah.

Ezekiel would seek to make it extremely clear that the judgment predicted in the Mosaic covenant was coming upon all in Jerusalem, with the hope that through the judgment Judah would see that the glorious God of judgment *is* Yahweh. He desired to be their God and wanted them to live as His people, no longer wandering astray from Him and defiling themselves (cf. 14:11).

Ezekiel was commanded to dramatize another message of the forthcoming exile of the present inhabitants of Jerusalem. This portrayal should have been understood by all the exiles, for Ezekiel played the role of one going into exile by digging through the wall of his house, and going out alone, carrying his meager necessities in a bag. If this picture did not prick their memories of the sadness of their exile experiences and the clarity of its meaning, Ezekiel proceeded to announce the interpretation of this symbolic act so that it could in no way be misunderstood. The people of Jerusalem *were* going to go into captivity and so would Zedekiah, their prince. Then Ezekiel portrayed the anxiety of the residents of Judah as they faced the desolation upon the land (12:1-20).

Having explicitly set forth the message of the coming judgment upon Jerusalem and Judah, Ezekiel proceeded to undermine the support for continuing optimism among the people. A proverbial saying was circulating in Jerusalem which declared: "The days are prolonged and every vision faileth" (12:22), or, in other words, "All the prophecies we have heard about coming judgment have perished and will not occur." God's long-suffering was employed as an argument against His faithfulness and immutability because they erroneously believed that a God of love could not judge. Others, who did believe that God was faithful to His pronouncements, rationalized by declaring the fulfillment of these judgments to be in the future. Thus they believed there was no cause for alarm in their day. In contrast to such optimism, Ezekiel replied that the judgment which he had announced would come to pass during their lifetime. God is faithful to His word. Judgment was imminent. When God dispersed His people among the nations, then they would know that He is Yahweh (12:20-28).

"But," the Israelites might have argued, "we have listened to the prophets and prophetesses and they have told us that this is a time of peace. No judgment is coming." Ezekiel retorted by announcing that they had relied upon prophets who spoke from their own hearts and spirits and who had seen no visions from God. These prophets had declared a false message of hope and peace; they had not spoken God's message. As a result they had not prepared the nation for the judgment which was coming (13:1-23).

Then the leaders of Israel in exile came to Ezekiel to inquire what the Lord's will was. But they came with hearts hardened through the idolatry fostered by the false prophets. They did not really want to know God's will, and they would only do it if it benefited their selfish desires. God answered them by encouraging them to repent and to turn to Him, or to be judged (14:1-11).

Another misconception lay in the hope that perhaps a single righteous man in their generation could exert enough influence with God to deliver others along with himself. Such an idea was erroneous, declared Ezekiel. Even if Noah, Job, or Daniel were in the midst of this people, their righteousness would deliver their own souls, but none other. Each man was responsible for himself (14:12-23).

Having treated these baseless rationalizations of the people and having demonstrated that the judgment of God was imminent and instructive, to cause them to know that He is Yahweh, Ezekiel summarized God's message of judgment in a parable (15:1-8). Israel was like a wild vine found in the forest which was unprofitable for the normal uses of wood, except that of burning. Therefore, just as this vine was fit only for consumption by fire, so also Israel was fit only for the divine fire of God's judgment.

The figure of Israel as a vine is employed elsewhere in the Old Testament, often denoting the idea of Israel as a chosen vine, planted and cared for by God (cf. Is 5:1-7; Jer 2:21; Ho 10:1). Having likened Israel to the vine, it is almost as if Ezekiel heard someone say that it was not fair that Israel be judged since she was the chosen vine, and God should care for her. Ezekiel answered through an allegory that God had continually cared for Israel. Having found her as a castaway infant, He rescued, wooed, married, and adorned her. But she became unfaithful, and, as a harlot, she prostituted herself with other nations in following after their gods as her lovers. Throughout her history she had rebelled against Yahweh, and her wickedness had become even worse than that of Sodom and Samaria before her. Therefore God was perfectly just in bringing judgment upon her. He promised at her birth that she would be judged if she disobeyed His covenant with her (cf. Lev 26, Deu 30). Though the situation looks extremely bleak at this point, God reminded the exiles that He would be faithful to His promise of restoration (Deu 30) in the future just as He would be faithful to His threats of judgment (Eze 16:1-63).

In light of the previous allegory, one might have complained that the present generation was being judged because of Israel's past rebellious history, so Ezekiel presented a riddle in chapter 17 which emphasized the rebellion of the present generation against Yahweh by seeking security and help from Egypt. There was no hope in seeking help from Egypt nor in following Judah's present ruler, Zedekiah; there was only a future hope in the restoration of God's Kingdom and His righteous King, the Messiah. Zedekiah *would* fall, and the remnant would be scattered.

In light of this discussion of Israel's history, Ezekiel treated another major misconception which appeared to be prevalent among Israel. "What is the use of repenting?" felt the people of Ezekiel's day. "Had God not said that He would visit 'the iniquity of the fathers upon the children unto the third and the fourth generation of them that hate me?'" (Ex 20:5; 34:7; Deu 5:9). If we are judged, it is because of our fa-

41

thers' sins. What can we do about it? Even if we repent, it will not help."

To refute this concept, God stated that each man was responsible for his own deeds. Ezekiel showed how this principle of individual responsibility applied to the misconception of the people: a righteous father does not make his son righteous; neither does a wicked father make his son wicked. A person lives or dies according to his own decision to obey or disobey God's ways (cf. Deu 30:15-20). The judgments being pronounced upon Israel by Ezekiel and the other prophets were the judgments enumerated in the Mosaic covenant for those who disobeyed its stipulations (cf. Lev 26; Deu 28). Though the announcements had been primarily on a national plane, each individual was responsible for himself as to whether *he* would live or die. God declared that it is His desire that everyone live. That is the reason He gave the commandments of the Law so that everyone would know how to live as God meant life to be lived. If one lived according to these righteous ways of God, he would be declared righteous and live. If he disobeyed God's righteous ways and broke the covenant, God promised that he would die as a result of his unrighteous deeds (Eze 18:1-31).

The penalty here was physical death, not eternal death. One's eternal salvation was not the issue. Eternal salvation was by faith in the Messiah in Old Testament times, just as it is today. Salvation never was attained by keeping the stipulations of the Law, neither then nor now. The Mosaic covenant demonstrated how one who already had entered into a relationship with Yahweh was to continue to live.

This entire section (chaps. 12-19) is concluded with a final dirge upon the recent rulers of Judah: Jehoahaz and Jehoiachin. The genuine rulers of Judah were gone. Since the recognized ruler of Israel, Jehoiachin, was already in Babylon, the people were not to look to unofficial leaders such as Zedekiah. Judgment was imminent!

MONODRAMA: GOING INTO EXILE (12:1-20)

In Deuteronomy 29:1-4 Moses reminded Israel just prior to the conquest of the land of Canaan that though they had observed the Lord accomplish many great and marvelous signs and wonders since they left Egypt, still they had not fully understood the significance of God's acts. Isaiah exhorted the nation of Israel (Is 6:9-10) that they had not yet comprehended God's workings. Though they had ears and eyes, they had not really heard and seen. Ezekiel picked up this same refrain (Eze 12:1-2). Though the prophets had announced judgment over and over again in light of the Mosaic covenant, Israel had continued to rebel, refusing to listen or to understand the message. Apparently they had not "seen" or "heard" the symbolic acts and messages of warning from their own contemporary, Ezekiel. Therefore God admonished Ezekiel to act and to proclaim his message of judgment with greater simplicity (12:1-3).

Ezekiel played on the concept of "seeing" and "hearing." He was to present a monodrama "before their eyes" (a phrase repeated seven times in five verses) as a "sign" (v. 6, NASB) to them. If they did not *see* the message in his symbolic act (vv. 3-7), he would then interpret it in verses 8-16 so that they could also *hear* it. In the daytime Ezekiel was told to transport from his residence the things that exiles would take with them. Perhaps Judah would see in Ezekiel a picture of themselves as a rebellious people who were going into captivity. In the evening Ezekiel was to hide his face as he went through a hole dug in the wall of his house.

If ever the exiles in Babylon should have understood the message, it was then. They all had gone through the misery of being torn from their beloved homeland and carried away into the strange land of Babylon. Ezekiel's monodrama should have brought back painful memories. But to make sure that they truly understood this message, Ezekiel reinforced it with an oral interpretation in verses 8-16. His "burden" (v. 10, a term used for a difficult message that a prophet must deliver) concerned the prince of Jerusalem, Zedekiah, and all the house of Israel. Ezekiel had been dramatizing Judah's approaching captivity. The daytime scene depicted the deportation of the people. The evening scene portrayed Zedekiah and his army. Second Kings 25:1-22 and Jeremiah 39:1-10; 52:1-10 recount the fulfillment of this prophecy. As Ezekiel went out in darkness through a hole dug in the wall, covering his face, so Zedekiah and his army would flee from the Babylonians during the night through the small gate in the king's garden, sneaking out so no one would see them. However, God declared that Zedekiah would be blinded and then brought as a captive to Babylon where he would die. Zedekiah's army would be scattered, and many would die by the sword. These events were fulfilled in 2 Kings 25:5-21 and Jeremiah 39:6-9; 52:8-11.

The message of coming judgment by means of the exile should have then been transparent. It would be necessary for God to execute this threatened judgment "in order that they shall know that I am Yahweh" (see Eze 12:15, 16, 20). God's judgments are messages to teach people of His mighty person and thereby cause them to turn to Him in faith and obedience. Thus, judgment is for good!

Scene two is observed in verses 17-20. Ezekiel was to eat bread and drink water (the meager portions of those being besieged), shaking anxiously in order to demonstrate the anxiety that those going into exile would experience. Then they would realize that their iniquity was full and that the land would become desolate because of their violence. This also was to cause them to know that the Lord *is* Yahweh.

Ezekiel declared that God would leave a remnant in Jerusalem and Judah at the time of the Babylonian destruction of Jerusalem. Perhaps these were the ones mentioned in 2 Kings 25:12-22 and Jeremiah 39: 10; 52:10. The rest of captive Judah would be a testimony to the nations where they would go. They would demonstrate God's faithfulness in keeping His word to judge the abominations which they had committed against Him. By this testimony the nations also would *know that Israel's God was Yahweh,* the only true God. Since the nation of Israel had failed to fulfill her vocation as a witness of the person and work of Yahweh to all nations, now He would cause her to be that witness by His judgment upon her.

GOD'S JUDGMENT IS CERTAIN (12:21-28)

Ezekiel's monodrama had shown that there comes a time in God's program when sin is full and judgment must come. But apathy concerning the warnings of the prophets continued. God's long-suffering delay of judgment, graciously giving time for Israel to repent and turn to Him, had been misinterpreted. Israel had demonstrated that she had not genuinely heard Ezekiel's message or that of the other prophets. Two forms of indifference had arisen: the attitude that (1) the prophecies of judgment would never occur, as seen in the proverb: "The days are prolonged, and every vision faileth" (v. 22); or (2) the judgment would be in the distant future (v. 27). The first argument maintained that the nonfulfillment of the judgment announced by such great prophets as Isaiah, Micah, and Zephaniah clearly indicated that those indictments were false. And since Ezekiel was proclaiming that same judgment, why should Judah listen to him? (Cf. the same apathy in 2 Pe 3:4.) Such reasonings denied the long-suffering of God and demonstrated that Judah did not believe in the inspired Scripture or in an immutable and faithful God. Yahweh's response to this apathy was twofold: (1) false divinations and visions which some prophets had declared in the past would cease—the people were not to base their hope on them; and (2) Yahweh's word would be performed exactly as He had spoken it, and *in their day*.

The second form of apathy toward God's judgments seemed to arise among those who still believed that God would do what He had declared, but who felt that it obviously would not be in their day. They thought these judgments must be for the future. To this Yahweh replied: "I will no longer wait. I will execute My judgments now."

WOE TO THE PROPHETS AND PROPHETESSES (13:1-23)

In Yahweh's response to the apathy of Israel in 12:24, He implied that such indifference to His judgment had been fostered by the false visions and divination of some prophets among Israel. The prophets had said that a time of peace was before the people. The prophets were helping the people "paint their houses" as if no calamity faced them at all (13:10). The "settle down and live" philosophy was prevalent.

The prophets of Israel were many. Though we may think that the only prophets who spoke in the Old Testament times were the great prophets of Scripture, the fact is that the majority of prophets seemed to be those who went along with the thinking of the day, declaring the messages that the people wanted to hear. These were the prophets of 12:24 who were seeing false visions.

These false prophets were foolish men, as are all those who listen to men rather than to God. Their messages stemmed from their own hearts and desires (13:2). They had either received no visions from God (v. 3) or they had seen false visions, resulting in empty words (vv.

45

6-8). They audaciously said Yahweh had spoken when He had not (vv. 6-7), thereby misusing the divine formula of authoritative speech: "Thus says the LORD." These prophets had not only led Israel astray by their false messages and actions (v. 10), but they themselves were walking (or living) according to the standard of their own spirit rather than according to the Spirit of God. These prophets were counterfeits in the role of religious leadership, for the sinful nature and spirit of man would certainly never proclaim God's ways.

It might seem that these prophets had been rather harmless. After all, they really had not hurt anyone. It was just a case of being misled and of making a small mistake. This, however, was not God's perspective. Because of their failure to speak the truth, they had failed to prepare Israel for the time of judgment, bringing destruction upon the people and the land as foxes in waste places (vv. 4-5). Rather, they had led Israel astray (v. 10). For these reasons the false prophets would be judged.

The judgment of the false prophets was threefold: (1) They would be cut off from the assembly (or place of counsel) of God's people, losing any and all authority, respect, and opportunity for counsel they might have ever had. (2) They would not be written in the writing of the house of Israel. There are two normal understandings of the phrase "the writing of the house of Israel." Some have taken it to refer to the "book of life" (cf. Rev 3:5; 20:15), with its eternal implications. Others take this to refer to the registers of the citizens of Israel such as are found in Ezra 2:62 and Nehemiah 7. Since the context of the phrase is that of the prophets being cut off from their place in the council of Israel and not returning to the land, it seems that the latter view of the registry was most likely meant; in other words, these erring prophets would be excommunicated from the citizenry of Israel. Now, if they were cut off from the people of God and had no future hope of restoration to the land—which in their case referred to the return from the Babylon captivity— there was the possibility that they might not participate in the "book of life" either. However, the stated purpose of their judgment in verses 9 and 14 was to bring them to the realization that the Lord is Yahweh. If that occurred, then it would seem that they still had a chance to be in the "book of life." Perhaps the issue was similar to the line of Malachi's argument in Malachi 3:16-18. (3) They would not reenter the country of Israel, a reference to the return from captivity, not the future restoration.

Yahweh's anger was against them in judgment so that when the storm of God's judgment hit Judah, it also would fall upon these prophets. God's purpose of judgment again was to bring the prophets to a realization that He *is* Yahweh (vv. 9, 14).

Then Ezekiel turned his attention to the prophetesses of Judah (13: 17-23). This passage is unique in that it is the most complete discussion of prophetesses in the Old Testament, though negative in tone. Ezekiel stated that flattering divinations were the primary work of the prophetesses of his day, a practice common to women in the ancient Near East.

These women had prophesied from their own hearts (v. 17), seeing empty visions and divinations (v. 23). They were lying to the people, who, the Lord added, were listening to their lies, though they refused to listen to the true messages of God through His genuine prophets (v. 19*b*). Such lies were causing people to die who would otherwise live, and those to live who otherwise should die. For example, they encouraged violence against the righteous and failed to enforce the judgments of the Mosaic covenant upon the wicked. The major concentration of their ill practices was in the realm of sorcery or witchcraft.

Varying opinions have been expressed concerning the significance of the terms and practices described in verses 18-23. Almost all will agree that these women practiced some form of sorcery or witchcraft, though the exact ritual they employed is unknown elsewhere. The bands (not pillows as once thought because of weak translations) on their wrists, the long veils worn over their heads, and the bits of bread and handfuls of barley all appear to be methods whereby the women would hunt or seek out God's people to kill them through their magic or to keep the wicked alive. These practices were unknown in Canaan in Ezekiel's day. However, in Babylon the magical practice of employing tied cloths or bands symbolized the magician's possession of a person, similar to the classical voodoo procedure. The veils were like cloaks worn by women when they engaged in such ritual, while the barley and bread are thought to be other avenues of witchcraft. Some have thought that the barley and bread were the payment required to hunt a person, but the context seems to imply that they were also a means of causing people to live or die, whether in voodoo fashion or as a poison. These concepts are conjecture not based on specific data. However, since some of these practices were found in Babylon at that time, and since Judah was greatly influenced by Babylon, it is certainly plausible that these women were engaged in Babylonian witchcraft and magic. In addition to their practices, they spoke lies which disheartened and intimidated the righteous (v. 22a). Yahweh made it known, however, that these prophetesses had brought this grief upon His people, strengthening the wicked's rebellion and encouraging him in his wicked ways (v. 22b).

Leviticus 19:26 strictly forbids the practice of witchcraft. The prophet therefore announced Yahweh's judgment upon these women. God would tear off the wristbands and long veils which they wore when they sought souls (persons).

A questionable term is used in verse 20. It has been translated "birds," "flying things," or "to flee." There are three meanings of this term in the Hebrew language: (1) "to bud or blossom," (2) "to break out," and (3) "to fly." Since the normal usage of the word is either "blossom" or "break out," the author is surprised that the majority have chosen the other meaning, "to fly" or "birds," which is employed nowhere else in the Old Testament. It seems that the concept of seeking persons to inflict them with an outbreaking of some disease is the more common practice of witchcraft than to try to employ the meaning of "flying thing" which really makes no sense in this context.

Therefore it appears that these women were using their magical powers to inflict diseases which ultimately would kill people, or to cure diseased people who otherwise would die. God was saying that He would remove their magical powers and deliver His people Israel from their grasp (vv. 20-21, 23). These prophetesses would never again see their empty visions or divinations (v. 23). The purpose of God's judgment here was the same as stated above: to cause these women to know that He is Yahweh, with the hope that they would repent from their evil ways and turn to the Lord (v. 21c).

Yahweh had just stunned the exiles by declaring that they had been duped and led astray by the false prophets and prophesying women (chap. 13). Therefore, the elders of Judah in exile as representatives of the people of Israel (14:4*a*-6), had come to Ezekiel to inquire of the Lord just what His way was. This was ironical since Ezekiel and the other true prophets had been telling Israel of God's ways for some time. Ezekiel, in contrast to the false prophets, did the work of a true prophet by declaring to the people the messages of judgment and the need for repentance.

As these elders confronted Ezekiel, the Lord reminded him that they had followed the messages of the false prophets and had worshiped idols rather than Yahweh as the guiding force of their lives. These idols had continually been a stumbling block for the elders and the people of Judah whom they represented (vv. 4*a*-6). But even though these elders were idol worshipers, Yahweh would still entertain their inquiry concerning His ways. God always responds to the desire to know the right way, even from sinners and idolators.

Yahweh's answer was essentially threefold: (1) He had allowed the idols to grasp the elders' hearts until they were thoroughly convicted of their need to turn to Yahweh (vv. 4-5). (2) Since they had been estranged from Yahweh through following the false prophets and the idols they endorsed, it would then be necessary that the elders and people repent, turning to Yahweh from the idols and all the abominations they had practiced (v. 6). (3) If, however, they did not turn in repentance, Yahweh would judge them (vv. 7-11). Yahweh would set Himself against them before the nations (cf. the language and promise of Lev 20:2-6). He would make them a sign and proverb of His faithfulness to judge (Deu 28:36-37), and He would cut the nonrepentant off from the rest of the people of Israel (Eze 14:7-8). Again, the purpose of Yahweh's judgment was to cause them to know that He *is* Yahweh, the One who is faithful to His promises to judge and bless in light of the Mosaic covenant.

In case the elders would quickly reply that they had been duped and their plight was really the fault of the prophets, Ezekiel reminded them that God purposely deceived the prophets in order to bring these prophets to the depths of conviction of their sinful ways (cf. vv. 4-5 above). Yahweh had already judged the prophets (cf. chap. 13), and the elders (or inquirers) also would bear the same punishment for their iniquity. It does not pay to follow the false prophets.

God announced this message to these elders to bring them to repentance, because Yahweh's great desire and purpose for the people of Israel was that they no longer would wander astray from Him, but rather turn to Him and be His people, as He created them to be, and He would be their God (cf. Ex 19:5-6; Lev 26:12; Jer 7:23; 31:33; Eze 11:20; 36:28). What love and long-suffering were demonstrated in Yahweh's call to His people through Ezekiel!

THE RIGHTEOUS ABLE TO DELIVER ONLY THEMSELVES (14:12-23)

Ezekiel then challenged the whole nation to remember several basic principles from the Mosaic covenant. The nation or land which sinned and acted unfaithfully against Yahweh would be cut off from blessing (cf. Lev 26:22-26). Yahweh is faithful to this basic principle.

Then it is almost as if the people hopefully asked: "Is it possible that a great righteous man could, on the basis of his righteousness, cause God to spare the nation, or at least the individuals upon whom that man would have favor?" Ezekiel replied with another basic principle of God's Word: "No! Each individual is responsible for himself" (see vv. 14-21). In support of his statement, the prophet showed that not even one of the well-known righteous men (Noah, Daniel, Job) could rescue the wicked in Judah from three different types of judgment which would come upon her: evil beasts (Lev 26:22); the sword (v. 25a); or pestilence (v. 25b).

These three men were chosen as examples because the Scriptures declare each to be righteous before God (cf. Gen 6:9; Job 1:1, 8; 2:3; Dan 6:4-5, 22). These righteous men were able to deliver only themselves out of situations of judgment (cf. Gen 6-9; Job; Dan 1, 5-6) and had very little effect on their own contemporaries. Likewise, none of these men would be able to deliver anyone other than themselves—not even their own children—from the judgment Ezekiel announced (cf. Lev 26: 22-26). Each person is responsible for himself before God.

Since some of the exiles were questioning the justice of God in executing such judgment upon those living in Jerusalem, the prophet reminded them that there would be a remnant of those from Jerusalem who would be sent to Babylon to join them (Eze 14:22). As the exiles would watch this remnant, the wickedness of this group would be obvious. Then the exiles would be comforted that God was right in His execution of judgment upon Jerusalem and Judah (cf. Eze 12:16; 6: 9-10). God's justice would be vindicated.

ISRAEL: A VINE FIT ONLY FOR BURNING (15:1-8)

In case there were any questions left in the minds of Ezekiel's hearers concerning the certainty of God's coming judgment upon Jerusalem, the prophet summarized the judgment and its reason in three parables. The first parable of the wild vine is given in chapter 15. A wild vine when compared with the other trees of the forest is seen to be useless for the normal functions of wood, with one exception. Though it is not suitable for normal work, nor strong enough to form a peg upon which to hang some utensil, it is suitable as fuel for a fire. As it was not fit for normal work before burning, it surely will not be fit for any task after its complete consumption by fire.

The interpretation of this parable is given in verses 6-8. Israel was the wild vine. Just as the vine was unsuitable for anything but burning, so Israel was only suitable for the burning fire of God's judgment. She would be entirely consumed. Even this had its purpose, for judgment was coming in order to demonstrate to Judah that God is Yahweh, the One who will be faithful to His declarations, even those of judgment. Why would she be judged? Because Israel had acted unfaithfully to Yahweh, resulting in ineffectiveness as "God's people" and as the "instrument of blessing" that Yahweh created her to be. God's judgments are not arbitrary. They are the exercise of His faithfulness to the divine standards of justice as seen in the Mosaic covenant.

JERUSALEM: THE HISTORY OF A HARLOT (16:1-63)

The figure of the vine probably reminded Ezekiel's hearers of the previous prophetic employments of this imagery (cf. Is 5:1-7; Jer 2:21; Ho 10:1-4) in which Israel was pictured as a chosen vine of Yahweh.

51

If Israel was a choice vine, why then should Yahweh burn her? Should He not instead be caring for her?

Ezekiel replied that God had cared for and loved Israel. Judgment was coming because Israel had turned from His love and care and had become a prostitute by following after and giving herself over to other nations and their gods. To demonstrate this, Ezekiel employed the figure or parable of a woman who became the bride of Yahweh and then committed adultery. Through this figure he succinctly recounted the history of Israel's abominations.

This symbol of a harlot specifically refers to Jerusalem and is significant. Though in this chapter Jerusalem represents the nation of Judah as her capital, Jerusalem also represents here the nation from the time of David forward. The key to the whole chapter is in verse 2: "Cause Jerusalem to know her abominations." This section does exactly that by recounting the history of Jerusalem's (and Israel's) sins.

The Circumstances of Jerusalem's Birth (16:3-5). The land of Canaan was the land which gave birth to Jerusalem as the capital of the nation of Israel. The reference to Jerusalem's father as an Amorite and her mother as a Hittite (cf. vv. 3, 45) has caused much debate. When treating a figure of speech, the interpreter should be careful neither to make the figure "walk on all fours" nor to give expanded interpretations of every facet of the image. Here Ezekiel is only emphasizing the place of Israel's and Jerusalem's origin. Their birth took place in Canaan, which is also known biblically as the land of the Amorites (especially when the hill country is being emphasized, as in the case of Jerusalem) and the land of the Hittites (cf. Gen 10:16; 15:16; Num 13:29; Jos 5: 1; 7:7; 24:15, 18; 1:4; Amos 2:10).

Jerusalem's birth was as terrible and despicable as a newborn child left in its blood, uncared for, and cast aside in a field as an unwanted infant. Her birth, as Israel's capital, occurred during the time of the conquest of Canaan and the judges, a period of turmoil, chaos, anarchy, and apostasy. The people of the nation were formed by Yahweh in Egypt and received their constitution at Mount Sinai, and their homeland (as promised in Gen 12:7) with the conquest of Joshua. But the actual birth of the created nation took place in Canaan, as did the birth of Jerusalem, her capital. In each case, the city and the nation were born in a chaotic religious and political situation.

Yahweh Loves and Marries Jerusalem and Israel (16:6-14). The parable explains that Yahweh found Jerusalem (Israel) in this despicable condition (cf. vv. 3-5), and in love He rescued her and enabled her to live. At the time of the kingdom under David, God took hold of Jerusalem (and Israel) and brought her to Himself as His bride. He entered into the marriage covenant (v. 8; cf. Pr 2:17) with her, and poured upon her the marriage gifts of the bridegroom (vv. 10-13; cf. Gen 24:53; Ps 45:14-15; Is 61:10). He made her a glorious and beautiful city and nation, and promoted her to royalty during the united kingdom under David and Solomon (cf. Lam 2:15), so that she became the dominant nation of the ancient Near East at that time. She became renowned among the nations for her beauty (cf. 1 Ki 10).

The covenant mentioned in 16:8 is thought by many to refer to the Mosaic covenant, the constitution of the nation of Israel. The basic essence of the term "covenant" in the midst of this figure is simply that of a marriage contract, showing the union that has been made between Yahweh and Jerusalem (Israel). Verses 59-63 imply that the covenant of verse 8 may also refer to the Mosaic covenant, which Yahweh made with the nation of Israel in her youth and which she now has violated, as the "marriage contract" between Yahweh and Israel.

Jerusalem's (Israel's) Prostitution with Other Lands and Gods (16:15-34). "But you trusted in your beauty" (v. 15, NASB). This was the beginning of the downfall of the nation. The peak of prosperity, wealth, and world fame had been reached during Solomon's reign. But it was exactly at that same time that the nation and her capital began to decline through trusting in the blessings and prominence which Yahweh had given her, rather than continuing to trust in Him. Solomon let his desire for preeminence lead him away from the Mosaic covenant (Deu 17:14-20) and toward devotion to the gods of his many wives (1 Ki 11:1-13). Jerusalem and the nation began to "fornicate" with the nations. That which was begun during Solomon's reign continued throughout the history of Israel and Judah. These two nations built high places to foreign gods, worshiping local and foreign idols, and sacrificing their children to them as in the worship of Molech (2 Ki 21:2-9).

53

The history of Jerusalem and the nation is filled with her spiritual adultery (cf. 1 Ki 12:28-33; 14:22-24; 16:30-33; 21:25-26; 2 Ki 15:35; 21:2-16; 2 Ch 24:17-19; 28:1-4). Jerusalem had forgotten those dreadful days of her youth when she was uncared for and a castaway, a time when she *was* nothing and *had* nothing (Eze 16:22). Israel prostituted herself with Egypt, trusting in Egypt for security rather than trusting in Yahweh (vv. 23-26; cf. 2 Ki 17:4; 18:21). She also played the harlot with Asshur (Assyria; Eze 16:28; cf. 2 Ki 17:3-12; 15:19-20) and Babylonian captivity—there was the possibility that they might not par- other gods were still not satiated. She went out and paid (with bribe and tribute) other nations and their gods to have relations with her, rather than the normal prostitute role of receiving pay from her lovers (Eze 16:30-34). "How weak and corrupt can her heart become?" asked Yahweh.

Jerusalem (Israel) Judged as a Prostitute (16:35-43). Since Jerusalem (Israel) was obscene in her nakedness, had become a prostitute with foreign nations and their gods through her idolatry and child sacrifice to idols (vv. 35-36), and had forgotten the gracious love and care that Yahweh had for her in her youth, the Lord would bring the judgment for adultery and murder upon her: death (vv. 38, 43b, cf. Ex 21:12, 14; Lev 20:10). His justice would be executed publicly before many women (v. 41, probably employed as a symbol of other rebellious nations in light of the context) through the instrumentality of her lovers (v. 39). Her lovers, the foreign nations, would strip her and leave her naked, cutting down her high places and taking her treasures. Then they would stone her (Lev 20:10), cut her down with the sword, and burn her houses with fire (cf. judgment for idolatry in Deu 13:12-16). The whole argument of the book of Ezekiel places this coming judgment at the fall of Jerusalem under the attacks of Babylon (cf. specifically chaps. 22-24). With the coming of the Babylonian captivity, the harlotry and idolatry with other gods would cease, never again to arise in Israel. This has been fulfilled, for in the Babylonian captivity Israel did turn from polytheism to monotheism, and the Jews have been a monotheistic people to the present day.

Jerusalem Was More Corrupt Than Samaria and Sodom (16:44-58). At this juncture Ezekiel shifted the imagery slightly to show the severity of Jerusalem's and Judah's wickedness through contrast with Samaria and Sodom. The land of Canaan (Amorite father and Hittite mother, cf. above) had given birth to three very corrupt daughters and their corresponding granddaughters (probably in this figure referring to the cities and environs which followed each of these major cities). A proverb had now become commonplace with respect to Jerusalem and Judah: "As is the mother, so is the daughter" (v. 44). This idiom is similar to our expression "like father like son." In other words, Jerusalem (Judah) had acquired the character of her mother, the land of Canaan, with all its perversion, idolatry, and religious syncretism.

But in addition, she had likewise become more wicked than her two sisters: Samaria (Israel, the Northern Kingdom from 931-722 B.C.) and Sodom (cf. Gen 10:19). Ezekiel played on the normal idiom for "older" (literally "greater") and "younger" (literally "smaller") when referring to these two cities. Samaria (representing the Northern Kingdom of Israel) was greater than Jerusalem (Judah) militarily and politically, while Sodom to the south had been smaller than Jerusalem. Sodom's sins are enumerated in Ezekiel 16:49 as pride, satisfaction in her prosperity ("bread"), false security, and lack of helping the poor and needy. These sins were at the heart of Sodom's problem in Genesis 18-19, which are there observed outwardly as sexual perversion (cf. this to the present analogy of Jerusalem in this chapter).

Though Sodom was very wicked, Jerusalem (Judah) had become more corrupt than she (16:47-48; 2 Ki 15:37; 16:6; 24:2; 2 Ch 28: 18-19; Eze 25:15). Likewise, Samaria was said to be only half as wicked as Jerusalem (Eze 16:51). In fact, Jerusalem's (Judah's) sins, by comparison, made Sodom and Samaria almost look righteous (v. 52). Therefore, as Sodom and Samaria had both been judged for their iniquity, so Jerusalem (Judah) would be also (vv. 50, 52-53, 58, cf. Lam 4:6). In addition, Jerusalem (Judah) would have no pride in the fact of her restoration over against these two cities, for those cities would also be restored to their former state in the land. The restoration of Sodom is not mentioned elsewhere in Scripture, and this presents an apparent problem since Sodom was said to have been totally destroyed (cf. Gen 19:24-27; Is 1:9). Though there is no biblically stated solution, certainly an omniscient God knows how this can occur.

Promise of Restoration (16:59-63). The recipients of Ezekiel's parable may have thought that Jerusalem (Israel) was so wicked that there was no future hope. Yet, just as Hosea demonstrated God's unfailing love for Israel (cf. Ho 3, 11), so Ezekiel concluded this chapter by reminding his listeners that God is always faithful to His covenants and promises, even when His people are unfaithful (cf. 2 Ti 2:13). Israel had despised her oath to keep the Mosaic covenant, and ignored its curse, through disobedience (cf. Ex 24:7-8; Deu 29:10-15).

When Yahweh completed the judgment, "then" (as the first word of Eze 16:60 should be rendered) He would remember His covenant which He made with Israel in the days of her youth (i.e., the Mosaic covenant). The difficult question in this section is to determine just which covenant is meant each time the term "covenant" is employed. In keeping with the analogy of this parable as seen in verse 8, the "covenant" would seem to be the Mosaic covenant. Yet the promise of restoration finds its origin in the covenant which God made with Abraham (Gen 12:1-3). Leviticus 26:42-45 and Deuteronomy 30 are very important at this juncture. Both are statements of the Mosaic covenant, and both give promises of restoration to Israel following her judgment by captivity. However, both of these passages base the hope of restoration on the Abrahamic covenant. Therefore, "my covenant" in verse 60 probably refers to the Mosaic covenant, in keeping with the parable; but, at the same time, that covenant in itself also refers to the Abrahamic covenant. This is made clear by the following clause of this verse: "I will establish unto thee an everlasting covenant." This cannot refer to the Mosaic covenant, for that covenant was never declared to be everlasting. In contrast, the Abrahamic covenant is everlasting (cf. Gen 17:7-8).

The ultimate restoration of Israel, based on the Abrahamic covenant, is promised in the remainder of this chapter. The word "covenant" in 16:61-62 refers to the Abrahamic covenant. In light of that covenant, Israel will be restored to prominence. At that time she will recognize the grace of God and become ashamed of her past wickedness (cf. 20:43; 36:31). Then her older and younger sisters (Samaria and Sodom) will become her daughters. What will be the result of the restoration? Israel will know that the Lord is Yahweh. God's faithfulness to His promises demonstrates again His faithfulness both to His promises to judge and also to bless. Verse 63 concludes the chapter with a glimpse of the promise of the new covenant (Jer 31:31-34) when Yahweh promises that Jerusalem (Israel) will no longer be humiliated, because He will have made atonement (covered) for those sins which she did.

THE RIDDLE AND ALLEGORY OF TWO EAGLES (17:1-24)

The long parable of Israel and Judah's idolatrous abominations in chapter 16 undoubtedly has raised additional questions and complaints in the minds of the exiles. Is it really fair that they should receive the judgment for all the past sins of the nation? Ezekiel answered the question on their minds by declaring that contemporary Judah would be judged because of her present lack of trust in Yahweh. Their leader, Zedekiah, had broken faith in his agreement with Nebuchadnezzar and had once again sought to rely upon Egypt rather than upon Yahweh. The present generation would be judged for its own sins.

Ezekiel made this announcement via a riddle and allegory of two eagles. The allegory is presented in verses 1-10, followed by its interpretation in verses 11-21. The chapter concludes with an epilogue in verses 22-24. A divine interpretation of the riddle is given in the context, emphasizing basic issues.

This riddle is addressed to the house of Israel (v. 2), a people that was still characterized by its rebelliousness (v. 12). The historical backdrop for the events described in this chapter may be found in 2 Kings 24:6-20, 2 Chronicles 36:8-16, Jeremiah 37, and 52:1-7.

The allegory and its interpretation are divided into two parts: the discussion of the first eagle and the discussion of the second eagle. The first eagle was declared to be Nebuchadnezzar, the king of Babylon (vv. 1-6, 11-14) who would remove the crest of the cedar with its young twigs and bring it to Babylon, the land and city of merchants. The cedar has Messianic connotations, as seen in Isaiah 10:33—11:1; Jeremiah 22:15, 23; and 1 Kings 10:27. In turn, the interpretation declared that the crest of the cedar referred to the king of Judah, Jehoiachin, who was taken captive along with other nobles by Nebuchadnezzar in 597 B.C. (v. 12; cf. 2 Ki 24:10-12). The place of captivity was Babylon, a land of merchants (v. 4b).

The change in the figure from the cedar to a vine is significant. The cedar, with its royal implications, was taken to Babylon, as in the captivity of Jehoaichin, the rightful king. Those left behind in Judah (or planted in the good land of Palestine; transplanted in vv. 8, 10) became a vine such as the one described in chapter 15. Nebuchadnezzar would place one from the royal line (v. 13, in reference to the "seed of the land" in v. 5) in the field of the seed, or Palestine (cf. vv. 22-23). Zedekiah (or Mattaniah; cf. 2 Ki 24:17; Jer 37:1), the youngest son of Josiah, was that one whom he placed as leader over those remaining in Judah in 597 B.C. Though Zedekiah was of the royal seed, he was neither recognized by Babylon nor by Judah as the rightful king; he was only a regent. Jehoiachin, the rightful king was now in Babylon. It is the remnant of Judah under the leadership of Zedekiah which is described as a vine that will never gain much height (i.e., the kingdom will never exalt itself).

The second eagle (vv. 7-10; 15-21) refers to Egypt (v. 15) to whom Zedekiah and Judah would send messengers for military aid when they rebelled against Nebuchadnezzar in 588 B.C. (v. 7) and break the covenant oath and agreement which Nebuchadnezzar established with Zedekiah when he placed him upon the throne of Judah in 597 B.C. (vv. 15b-16). "Will Zedekiah prosper in his rebellion?" the allegory asks in verses 9-10. "No," declares the divine interpretation. "He will be judged for breaking his covenant with Nebuchadnezzar" (vv. 16, 18) "and God's covenant with Moses" (see v. 19).

This judgment upon Zedekiah, the leader upon whom the exiles in Babylon have based their hope for a quick return to Palestine, is delineated in verses 16-21: (1) Egypt will be of no help when he turns to her (v. 17). (2) Yahweh will spread out His net and seize Zedekiah and bring him to Babylon (v. 20; cf. Eze 12:13). (3) Zedekiah's armies shall fall by the sword or be scattered (v. 21; cf. Eze 12:14). (4) Zedekiah shall die in Babylon (v. 16; cf. Eze 12:13). The purpose behind this judgment is, "and ye shall know that I the LORD [Yahweh], have spoken" (v. 21).

Ezekiel concluded this allegory with an epilogue (vv. 22-24). Even though the present king, Jehoiachin, and his regent, Zedekiah, had failed Yahweh by leading the nation into iniquity, thus bringing on the discipline of God, in the future Yahweh will establish the righteous King, the Messiah, upon the throne of David. The allegory in this chapter refers to a tender one cut out of the treetop of the cedar. It was shown above that this "cedar" has Messianic implications. Likewise, the "tender one" has its Messianic references (cf. Jer 23:5-6; 33:14-16; Is 11:1; Zec 3:8; 6:12-13). This is a new cutting from the top of the tree, not part of the previous "cutting" which was taken by Nebuchadnezzar to Babylon in verse 4. This is in keeping with the prophecy of Jeremiah 22:28-30 that the physical line of Coniah (Jehoiachin) will not sit on the throne of David (although his Descendant would). This new King, the Messiah, will be planted by God (not Nebuchadnezzar) in the land of Israel beside the high and lofty mountain, undoubtedly a reference to Mount Zion, the location of the Temple complex (Ps 2:6; Eze 20:40; Mic 4:1). Here this tender branch will become a mighty cedar—in contrast to the useless vine which depicted the nation under Zedekiah—which will be fruitful and under which every kind of fowl will reside. These birds appear to refer to the nations which will be gathered unto Yahweh, the Son of David, when He comes to rule upon the earth (Is 2:2-3). The allegory is concluded with a principle: It is God who raises up trees (contextually referring to kings and their nations) and brings them down, causing them to flourish or to wither. Yahweh is sovereign in the political affairs of this earth (cf. Dan 4:17, 32, 34-37).

EACH MAN SEEN AS LIVING OR DYING BY HIS OWN DEEDS (18:1-32)

At this point in Ezekiel's argument the exiles were probably thinking: "What hope do we have? If we are reaping the results of our fathers' sins of the past and those of our present rulers, what can we do about it? Even if we repent, it will not help us." This way of thinking already had begun to manifest itself in a proverb which was becoming famous: "The fathers eat sour grapes and the children's teeth are blunt (or dull)" (cf. Jer 31:27-30). In other words, what the father does always affects his children. Here the exiles applied the concept of heredity specifically to the area of their sin and guilt. "Unrighteousness or righteousness are always inherited," they declared (see vv. 1-2).

Yahweh responded by declaring that this proverb will cease, for the hereditary principle as the cause of wickedness or righteousness in invalid. Each man is responsible for himself before God, according as it is declared in the Mosaic covenant (Deu 24:16; cf. 2 Ki 14:6). God alone judges a man's righteousness or wickedness, and the man's state is determined by how he acts; each person decides to do iniquity or righteousness (vv. 3-4).

This was not the first time that Ezekiel had treated this issue. He already had alluded to it in his discussion of Israel's response to his warnings as her watchman in 3:16-21 and in his declaration in 14:12-20 that no righteous man could deliver another man from the judgment to come. He treats this matter one more time in 33:1-20.

It is essential to the understanding of this passage that the concept of life and death according to the Mosaic covenant be clearly understood. Ezekiel declared in 18:4 that "the soul that sinneth, it shall die." Yahweh was not talking about spiritual life and death in this passage, for the whole discussion of this book is seen in light of the Mosaic covenant. This covenant makes it very clear over and over again that the one who obeys will live physically, and the one who disobeys the covenant will die physically (cf. Lev 26; Deu 28:58-66; 30:15-20). It is within this context that life and death are understood in this chapter.

In the Old Testament, eternal life was gained only by faith in the coming Messiah (see Gen 15:6). The Mosaic covenant, as the constitution of Israel, was given to a people who already were in a relationship with God. It was not given to place an individual in that relationship, but rather to show how a person in a relationship with God was to live. God, the Creator of life, was declaring to His children, whom He loves, how life was to be lived at its best.

So that the exiles would understand what he was saying, Ezekiel gave three examples. The first is as follows: The righteous man will live by his righteous deeds (vv. 5-9). The righteous works which a righteous man is to perform are enumerated; all are from the Mosaic covenant: (1) He does not engage in idolatrous worship by eating on the pagan mountain high places or looking to idols (cf. Deu 12:2, 13-14). (2) He does not defile his neighbor's wife (cf. Ex 20:14; Lev 20:10; Deu 22:22) nor engage in fornication (Lev 15:24; 18:19; 20:18). (3) He does not maltreat people by failing to restore his pledge of debt (Ex

22:26-27), robbing (Ex 20:15; Lev 19:13), refusing to give food to the hungry and clothes to the naked (Deu 15:11; cf. Is 58:7), charging and receiving interest (Ex 22:25; Deu 23:19-20; cf. Is 24:2), or participating in injustice between men (Lev 19:15-16, 35-36; Deu 25:13-16). (4) He walks (or lives) according to the stipulations of the Mosaic covenant in order to do the truth (Lev 18:1-5; Deu 11; 26:16-19). If a man does these things, Ezekiel declared, on the basis of Yahweh's authority, this man shall surely live (cf. Deu 30:15-20).

The second illustration: A righteous man's violent son shall not live (Eze 18:10, 13, 18). The violent deeds which this son performs are all of the acts listed above, from which the righteous man refrains. When he does these things, the judgment of the covenant (cf. Lev 26) will be upon him, his blood shall be upon him (i.e., death). The righteousness of his father is not inherited; it will not deliver him.

The third case: The righteous son of a violent father shall live (vv. 14-18). Though the father's works are wicked according to the Law, when his son performs those righteous acts listed in verses 5-9, he shall not die because of his father's iniquity, but he shall surely live. Why? Because he obeyed the covenant and is righteous (or right) according to its standards.

At this point Ezekiel posed the rhetorical question his opponent might raise: "Why does not the son bear the iniquity of his father?" Yahweh's reply (vv. 19-24) sets forth several important principles: (1) When a son (or anyone) keeps the Mosaic covenant and thereby executes righteousness, he shall live whether his father does or not. (2) The sinner will always die. (3) A son does not bear his father's sins, nor does the father bear the son's sins (though they might suffer from each other's sin). (4) The righteous live because of their righteousness; the wicked die because of their wickedness. (5) If the wicked turns from all his sin and keeps the Mosaic covenant, he will live. None of his sins will then be remembered against him to cause death. (6) Yahweh does not delight in the death of the wicked; rather, He desires that the wicked turn to Him and live (cf. 18:32 with 2 Pe 3:9, which treats spiritual life and death by the same principle). (7) If the righteous man turns from his righteousness, which is based on the Law, and sins by disobeying the Law, then he surely will die. His righteousness will not be remembered.

"But you are not fair and equitable," responded Israel (see vv. 25, 29). "My ways are equitable and fair," declared Yahweh. "Your ways are not fair" (see vv. 25-29). "Your hereditary principle does not allow a person to change, but rather keeps him in his present condition or that of his parents."

Ezekiel summarized his argument in the final three verses (vv. 30-32) of this chapter: Yahweh would judge each individual according to his own ways (cf. Deu 24:16). In light of that fact, the Lord exhorted Israel to turn from her sins and obtain a new heart and spirit and live (cf. a similar discussion in Eze 11:19; cf. 36:26; 2 Ch 6:14, 36-42; Jer 29:10-14; 31:33; 32:39). It was necessary for Israel to change her heart from hardheartedness (Eze 2:4; 3:7; 6:9) to a new heart, ultimately given by God in the new covenant (cf. Jer 31:33; Eze 36:26). It is interesting to note that God coupled His announcements of judgment, both personally and nationally, with an invitation to repent and live. "Why should Israel die?" grieved the Lord who does not want even one person to die (18:31; cf. v. 23). "Turn and live!" declared Israel's God.

A DIRGE AGAINST THE RULERS OF JUDAH (19:1-14)

Ezekiel had finished his apologetic for the judgment of God. As a finale to this section of the book, Yahweh exhorted Ezekiel to take up a dirge against the princes (a frequent reference to kings) of Israel. The dirge was given through two figures: (1) a lioness and her whelps (vv. 1-9), and (2) a vine and its rods (vv. 10-14).

In the first figure, the lioness is a personification of the kingdom of Judah. The representation of the nation by a lion is not new (cf. Gen 49:9; Num 23:24; 24:9; Rev 5:5). The first whelp is Jehoahaz (vv. 3-4; cf. 2 Ki 23:30-34; 2 Ch 36:1-4), who is appointed by the people of Judah following the death of Josiah. The evil which he does (cf. 2 Ki 23:32) is here declared to be the devouring of mankind. He becomes known among the nations for his wickedness and is seized by

Pharaoh Necho and taken in fetters (as a captured lion) to Egypt in 608 B.C. There he dies.

Jehoiakim, Judah's next ruler, is not discussed, perhaps due to his natural death and the fact that his wickedness was not as great as that of his brothers. The next whelp is Jehoiachin (vv. 5-9; cf. 2 Ki 24:6-16; 2 Ch 36:8-10). Even though Judah's hope had perished (v. 5) with the deportation of Jehoahaz and the death of Jehoiakim, Jehoiachin is established on the throne of Judah. He likewise devours mankind and makes cities desolate through his roarings. The nations come against him as in a lion hunt and seize him and bring him to Babylon (2 Ki 24:8-15), where later he is released (2 Ki 25:27-30). Through this figure Ezekiel is demonstrating the wickedness of these last kings of Judah and, by implication, the judgment which they are helping to bring upon Judah through their wicked leadership.

The second figure (vv. 10-14) is that of Judah as the mother vine, another figure not uncommon to Ezekiel or the rest of the Old Testament (cf. Eze 15; 17:5-8). As a vine, the nation became prosperous and fruitful (at the time of the united kingdom under David and Solomon). The rods which came forth from the vine were her rulers, not a specific one. The scepter is commonly employed as a symbol of the king (cf. Gen 49:10).

The vine (Judah) at the time of Ezekiel had become withered by the heat of God's divine anger and was cast to the ground by the east wind (undoubtedly a reference to Babylon in light of the context of Ezekiel's warnings). Judah's kings, as observed in the first figure, were broken and withered. She would be transplanted to the desert (Babylon) and would have no one to rule her (following Jehoiachin and Zedekiah). This would be accomplished completely with the fall of Jerusalem in 586 B.C. In his dirge Ezekiel emphasized the fact that the rulers (the rods) had been the primary fire to devour Judah by their wicked ways (the similar emphasis in v. 7 above).

This is the final statement of this section: a dirge upon the rulers in general and the last kings in particular. As a result of wicked leadership, judgment was now coming upon the land. This section of Ezekiel demonstrates why it was coming. Judah had no more rationalizations to bolster her false hopes that the judgment would not come.

THE HISTORY OF ISRAEL'S CORRUPT LEADERSHIP
(20:1—23:49)

SUMMARY

Eleven months had passed since Ezekiel so eloquently shattered Judah's optimistic hope that judgment would not really come upon her. The leaders in the exile had put forth their best arguments as to why Jerusalem and Judah should be spared, but Ezekiel had rebutted each point. These eleven months were undoubtedly months of silence and despair.

Suddenly in the late summer of 591 B.C. the news of an Egyptian victory in the Sudan and Psammetichus II's potential victory march into Palestine reached the exiles. Zedekiah was looking to Egypt for help, as the leaders of Judah often did. Had not Egypt just demonstrated that she was capable of recovering Palestine as one of her vassals? Zedekiah repudiated his allegiance to Babylon in favor of Egypt somewhere between the end of 591 B.C. and the summer of 589 B.C. It was ill-timed in light of the pharaoh's illness in 589 B.C. and the resulting weakening of Egypt's potential power.

The query of the Jewish exilic elders was probably conceived in this historical context. Though they never expressed their question, it may well have been "Will Zedekiah's current overtures to Egypt succeed so that Nebuchadnezzar will be defeated soon, and we can return to our homeland?" Ezekiel's reply to the exiles implied that such a request was probably on their minds, though God refused to hear their direct inquiry.

Ezekiel's response to their unasked question was threefold:

1. Look at the history of Israel and observe that she and her leadership have persistently rebelled against God. The contemporary rulers of Judah are no different (chap. 20).
2. Be prepared for a final judgment upon Jerusalem, for it will be coming soon by the hand of Nebuchadnezzar. More captives will be brought to Babylon (chap. 21).
3. Why does the leadership deserve this judgment? Look at their abominations and corruption. They are so perverted that Yahweh cannot even find one leader to point His people to Him in order that He might spare them. Instead, the leaders have prostituted their realm through foreign alliances with nations which they hate.

The result: Judgment, for the sake of correction in seeking to bring Yahweh's people back to His ways (chap. 22-23).

THE PAST CORRUPTION OF ISRAEL AND HER LEADERSHIP (20:1-44)

A delegation from the Israelite leadership in the captivity came to Ezekiel at a time when there was a growing attempt by some segments of the Jerusalem population to cast off the yoke of Babylon by turning to Egypt, which was beginning to show some strength.

The phrase "to inquire of Yahweh" is an idiom frequently employed by the prophets to introduce a request for a prophetic audience in which individuals would ask a prophet to determine the outcome of a specific event. These representatives of the elders were making such a request. Their unasked query sought a positive reply to their hopes that Judah, with the potential aid of Egypt, would throw off the dominion of Babylon. Then they, the exiles, could return to Israel.

Yahweh refused to hear yet another query, for He only desired their repentance. In His omniscience He knew what they desired. He had repeatedly announced through Ezekiel in the preceding chapters that judgment was now inevitable and imminent. There was no hope in Egypt except in repentance. Therefore God would not listen to the elders' request. Yahweh declared, "Will you judge them, Ezekiel?" This phrase is tantamount to saying, "Set forth the case before them." God would recount for them, in a very factual way, what He previously declared in parables: Israel's history was one of rebellion against the Lord. A summary of Israel's history follows in verses 5 through 44.

It All Started in Egypt (20:5-9). Israel's case history ironically began in the land of Egypt, the same nation upon which she was presently relying. Though the creation of the nation of Israel covered the period of time from Jacob[2] through the conquest of the land of Canaan, there is a real sense in which Israel was "born" in Egypt. It was here that the people from whom the nation would be made came into being. It was here that Yahweh swore by an oath (which is the meaning of the phrase "lifted up the hand") that He would be Israel's God and that He would

2. There are three essential elements in the creation of the nation of Israel: (1) a *people,* who came into being in Egypt from Jacob's twelve sons; (2) a *government,* which was provided in the Mosaic covenant at Mount Sinai; and (3) a *land,* which was acquired in the conquest of Canaan.

bring them out from the oppression of Egypt into the land of Canaan (cf. Ex 3:13-18; *6:1-9;* Deu 7:6-11). It was also in Egypt that God's people first turned aside after idols and defiled themselves. Though Yahweh exhorted them to flee idolatry, Israel refused to listen and continued in pagan worship (cf. Lev 17:7; Jos 24:14; Deu 29:16-17; Lev 26:30; 18:3), setting a pattern which she found difficult to break throughout her history. Yahweh disciplined Israel through the oppressions in Egypt in order to turn her back to Himself and to encourage her not to establish these idolatrous habits, but to give a proper testimony of His name before the nations (cf. Ex 7:5-6; Ps 106:8-12). Instead, Israel became increasingly stubborn in her wicked ways.

The Exodus and the Mosaic Covenant (20:10-12). God's compassion responded to the cry of His people in Egyptian bondage and brought them out of Egypt under the leadership of Moses (Ex 12-14) as He had promised (cf. Gen 15:13-16). He took His people to Mount Sinai where they received their constitution: the Mosaic covenant. This covenant set forth the way in which they, as God's covenant people, were to live (cf. Deu 10:12-21). The sign and seal of this covenant was the Sabbath (cf. Ex 20:8-11; 31:13, 17; Neh 9:14), which portrayed the covenant maker, God, as the Creator, perfectly in keeping with the fact that He was presently creating a nation.

Rebellion in the Wilderness Wanderings (20:13-26). The generation which came forth from Egypt (20:13-16) rebelled against Yahweh in the wilderness. This was most vividly demonstrated in their refusal at Kadesh-Barnea to go in and take the land of Canaan which God had promised to give them (cf. Num 11, 13-14; Ps 106:13-15, 19-23). Also they rejected the Mosaic covenant and its stipulations; they would not walk in God's ways, the ways that God said were for their own good (cf. Deu 10:13). They profaned the sign of the covenant, the Sabbath, through failure to observe it (cf. Num 15:32).[3] Because of their sin, Yahweh disciplined them so that His name might not be profaned[4]

3. It is interesting to note here that there is no mention of the observance of the Sabbath from Deu 5 to 2 Ki 4.
4. In the ancient Near East a nation was closely associated with her god. If the nation was defeated in battle, scattered abroad, et. al., other nations would think that her god was unable to care for her. In this sense Israel profaned Yahweh by being in exile.

before other nations (cf. Num 14:11-16; Ps 106:24-26; Deu 1:34-35); that generation would not enter into the promised land.

Yet that judgment did not encompass the entire nation. Those under the age of twenty would live. God desired that they would walk in His ways (Eze 20:17-26). Though Yahweh warned this new generation not to walk in their parents' sinful ways, but rather to live according to the Mosaic covenant, they also rebelled in the wilderness (cf. Ps 106: 16-18, 28-46) just as their fathers had done (cf. Eze 20:24; Num 25: 2-9). Then God threatened to destroy the people entirely, but Moses interceded on their behalf (cf. Num 16:21-22; 17:9-11; Ps 106:23). Then Yahweh announced that He would disperse them among the nations (cf. Lev 26:33; Deu 28:64; 32:26-27; Ps 106:26-27) and cause Israel to live under the heathen statutes which were not designed for good. This concept is clarified by the context (Eze 20:26) which argues that God gave Israel over to the perverse ways and statutes of the nations around her that she might see that only God's ways were right (v. 39; cf. Ps 81:12; Is 63:17; Ro 1:24-25). However, Israel became more defiled through the abominable and corrupt practice of devoting her first-born children to pagan deities (a Canaanite practice and part of the foreign worship of Molech). Yahweh allowed this to drive Israel to the logical end of her perversion: astonishment at herself. Then she might realize that God was Yahweh and turn to Him (v. 26).

Rebellion in the Conquest and Settlement of the Land (20:27-29). Even though Israel blasphemed God in the wilderness by acting unfaithful toward Him, the grace and faithfulness of God still brought them into Canaan. In the Abrahamic covenant (Gen 12:7) God had promised that He would give Israel the land of Canaan. What God promises, He will perform. There in the land of Canaan, Israel continued to carry on her abominable practices at the "high place." The "high place" may refer to the high place at Gibeon which was a prominent religious place in Israel during her early worship in that land (cf. 1 Ki 3:4; 1 Ch 16:39; 21:29; 2 Ch 1:3, 13; 1 Sa 9). However, the religious center of the nation settled in Jerusalem under the reigns of David and Solomon.

Contemporary Israel (20:30-44). Contemporary Israel of Ezekiel's day was acting no differently than Israel had acted in the past. "Are you not defiling yourselves in the ways of your fathers by going after idols and offering up your sons?" asked Yahweh. "You have not repented nor changed at all. And you want to know if the judgment will be suspended? The answer is emphatically 'no!'" (see 20:20-31).

Then Ezekiel proceeded to outline God's future dealings with Judah according to His promises (20:32-44). This passage truly demonstrates God's grace. Despite Judah's wickedness and rebellion, God pursued her in order to accomplish His purpose for that nation (cf. Phil 1:6). Yahweh refused to let Judah be like the other nations as her spirit desired (v. 32). Rather, He would rule over her as a father, with a hand of discipline through the Babylonian exile (v. 33), though He would ultimately regather His people from Babylon (v. 34). He also announced that there would be another dispersion (in addition to the Babylonian captivity) into the "wilderness of the people" (v. 35) just like when He took Israel into the wilderness from Egypt (v. 36). This future dispersion of Israel would be for the purpose of disciplining her (through purging) in order to bring her into a covenant bond where she would finally know that God is Yahweh (vv. 37-38).

The covenant mentioned in this context appears to be the new covenant (cf. Jer 31:31-34). In verse 39 God declared that He would turn Israel over to her own ways if she so desired, but ultimately He would make sure that she no longer profaned His name. That would occur when He (1) accepted Israel, (2) restored her, and (3) set Himself apart (sanctified Himself) through the true witness Israel would give of Yahweh before the nations. The basis of this would be God's grace, not what Israel deserved by her evil ways (v. 44). Israel, in turn, would (1) serve Yahweh in the land of Israel, (2) worship Him with the required offerings, (3) acknowledge Yahweh and His faithfulness in keeping the Abrahamic covenant through restoring her to the land, and (4) genuinely come to Yahweh in contrition for her sins. This passage strikingly parallels Deuteronomy 30:1-10 and the new covenant of Jeremiah 31:31-34. In other words, verses 35-44 are describing a future dispersion and regathering, much in keeping with the prophetic concept of the Day of the Lord (cf. Joel 2-3).

The impending judgment by Babylon is described in three different ways: a fire burning the southern forests of Palestine, the slaughter of Jerusalem and Judah with an unsheathed sword, and the imminency of Nebuchadnezzar's coming.

The Burning of the Southern Forest (20:45—21:7). The southern forests of Palestine are those in the hill country of Judah. A parable pictures a fire that would consume the forest and not be extinguished. In case the exiles missed the significance of the parable, it was interpreted in 21:1-7, in which the judgment was likened to a sword which would affect both the righteous and the wicked in Jerusalem and Judah. Of necessity the repercussions of any judgment always touch everyone in a country—the righteous and the unrighteous. The distressing effects of this judgment were demonstrated through Ezekiel's drama. Everyone would faint and become weak-kneed when this judgment came, and it was coming!

A Song of Judgment (21:8-17). In the Hebrew text this section is in poetic form and may have been a common lament song sung in times of coming judgment, or a song sung by Ezekiel in light of these specific events. The song declares that a sharp and polished sword, placed in the hand of a warrior, would be wielded against God's people Israel. All would be touched by the sword, especially the leaders and kings of Israel (cf. vv. 12-13). They were the responsible ones who had led the nation astray by failing to lead her to God. The present offender was Zedekiah! Verse 13 is somewhat ambiguous in some English translations. The idea is that the sword had been tested and was capable of accomplishing its purpose against the king (the "scepter" or "rod") who was despising Yahweh. Perhaps the reference to the sword having a triple effect in verse 14 implies the three deportations of Judah. Two had already occurred in 605 and 597 B.C. The third and final deportation would occur in 586 B.C. When that one came, Yahweh would cause His wrath to cease.

Babylon Would Judge Jerusalem Now; Ammon Would Be Judged Later (21:18-32). Then the sword of the previous two sections was identified. The king of Babylon was pictured as standing at the fork in the road toward Canaan which lies near the ancient town of Riblah. Ammon and Judah had both conspired against Babylon in 593 B.C. Nebuchadnezzar was employing the common means of divination to determine which kingdom he should subdue first. First, there was the process of marking arrows with names, placing them in a quiver, whirling them about, and the first one to fall out was the answer of the god. Second, idols (teraphim) were consulted; and third, the liver of a dead sheep was examined, and the answer from a god was determined by the color and markings of the liver. It appears that Nebuchadnezzar employed all three methods with the same result: lay siege to Jerusalem. The inhabitants of Jerusalem thought that the divination must be incorrect. Yet Yahweh reminded Judah that He was using Babylon as His instrument of judgment because of Judah's iniquities. Zedekiah, Jerusalem's weak leader just prior to the Babylonian captivity, would be taken off the throne (vv. 25-26). "Overturn, overturn, overturn" in verse 27 is for the sake of strong emphasis in the Hebrew language, nothing more. Destruction was coming upon Jerusalem. Destruction and lack of leadership would continue until the Messiah came, to whom the scepter belongs, and to whom Yahweh would give it (v. 27).

This chapter closes with the announcement of future judgment by the sword upon Ammon. That judgment was not imminent; however, it would come. For the present, the drawn sword was returned to its sheath, in respect to Ammon's judgment (vv. 28-32).

VINDICATION OF YAHWEH'S JUDGMENT UPON THE LEADERS
OF ISRAEL (22:1-31)

Yahweh began with "Will you judge the city?" or "Set forth the case against the city." His purpose was to declare the specific reasons for the impending judgment. God wanted to make sure Israel understood why judgment was coming. Jerusalem's idolatrous leaders and the resulting abominations were the major reasons for her judgment.

"Jerusalem" Was Synonymous with the Leaders of Judah Since It Was Their Capital City (22:1-5). A summary of the leadership's abominations was made in these verses. Jerusalem, whose leaders were shedding blood indiscriminately, was described as confused and defiled by idols.

This wickedness was making Jerusalem the derision and mock of all the nations. When one follows the world's ways, the world often ends up laughing at him.

What Had the Leaders of Judah Done to Cause These Judgments (22:6-12)? Ezekiel delineated the evidence of the case: The leaders deliberately had broken the specific demands of the Mosaic covenant. Each one misused the strength of his position to have people put to death unjustly (v. 6, forbidden in Ex 20:13). The leaders treated their parents with contempt, ignoring the rightful honor and respect due to parents and the home (v. 7a, forbidden in Ex 20:12). Strangers were oppressed in Judah, and they did nothing about it (v. 7b, forbidden in Ex 22:21; 23:9). The leaders took advantage of and maltreated those without a defender: widows and orphans (v. 7c, forbidden in Ex 22:22-24; Deu 24:17). Judah's officials despised the holy things of God and His Sabbaths (v. 8, forbidden in Ex 20:8). The leaders fostered corrupt government and organized crime whereby they encouraged murder based on slanderous accusations (v. 9a; cf. Lev 19:16; 1 Ki 21). They engaged in pagan religious rituals, worshiping on the mountains and high places of the pagans (v. 9b, forbidden in Deu 12:1-3; 16:21-22). Judah's public officials had engaged in sexual perversion, being exhibitors, adulterers, and those committing incest (vv. 10-11, forbidden in Lev 20:10-21; 18:6-23). They employed bribery (v. 12a, forbidden in Ex 23:8; Amos 5:12; Deu 27:25), exorbitant taxes and interest rates (v. 12b, forbidden in Deu 24:6, 10-12; 23:19-20), and oppression (v. 12c). All this was aptly summed up in verse 12d: "But you have forgotten Me," declared the Lord. The above list is also a commentary on many government officials in the world and in our country today.

The Response of the Lord to the Rebellion by Judah's Leaders (22:13-22). Yahweh would remove all that Judah's leaders had gained through their evil practices. He would reveal the true attitude of their hearts and deeds of their hands. Despising His ways was despising Him. Therefore Yahweh would bring judgment to purify Judah and her leaders just as one would purify ore. Judah was likened to raw ore. Jerusalem was portrayed as the furnace (ignited by Babylon). Yahweh smelted the ore in the furnace. Judah and her officials then came forth as dross, that is, impure. Yet, through this judgment Yahweh made Himself known as the Holy God whose ways were to be obeyed. He revealed Himself through judgment to those who had forgotten Him. Judgment was for the good of these people since it caused them to understand who Yahweh is.

Would No Leader Take a Stand for God (22:23-31)? "Let Me be specific," declared the Lord. The leaders to whom the people of Israel should have come for help and direction in times of chaos—the prophets and priests—were the very ones who were oppressing them. In a time of impending judgment when they needed the blessing of true leadership, there was no one to stand. There was no blessing (rain) in the day of indignation.

With the exception of Jeremiah and Ezekiel, the prophets of the day (vv. 25-28) were like vicious lions devouring the people. They were taking the wealth and possessions of desperate people who were anxiously waiting for the prophets to give a word of encouragement from God. Probably these riches were taken in payment for the false prophecies which these counterfeit prophets gave. These prophets frequently announced that the nation should go to war when God had not so directed, causing many warriors to be slain, which increased the number of widows in the land. The empty "visions" of these prophets were very attractive (whitewashed) so that the people did not discover the lies that were spoken. The prophets attributed their messages to God, although God had not spoken. These false prophets find their counterpart among many contemporary ministers and religious leaders.

The priests (v. 26) did violence to the Law of God (Mosaic covenant) by disobeying and disregarding it (e.g., Sabbaths). Instead, they had misused (polluted) God's holy ways so that no one knew right from wrong. The truth of God was perverted by what they taught. There were no absolutes; all was relative. Instruction in the true Law was obviously lacking.

The officials of the land acted like ravenous wolves devouring the people for their own gain (v. 27). Regrettably the common people followed the ways of their leaders—ways of extortion, robbery, and social and legal injustice (v. 29). What chaos!

God was desperately looking for a man to step forth and be a leader who would intercede before Him in behalf of the nation of Israel at this

72

point in her history, just as Moses had done in his day (cf. Ps 106:23), *but He could not find anyone!* (v. 30). The whole nation was corrupt! Therefore, the fire of God's wrath would be poured out. The ways of the nation would be placed on their heads, that is, they would be held accountable for their deeds (v. 31).

A SUMMARY PARABLE OF THE POLITICAL PROSTITUTION OF THE NATION ISRAEL (23:1-49)

Ezekiel undoubtedly assumed that his listeners remembered a previous parable that he had delivered in chapter 16. This author makes the same assumption. The two chapters are similar, with the exception of their emphasis. In chapter 16 the emphasis was upon Israel's religious adultery. Here in chapter 23, the emphasis is upon her political prostitution. She is represented as a nation always seeking to allure the other nations to love her so that she might reap the benefits of those relationships. Yet, all the time that she is intimate with them, she really despises them.

Identification of the Figures (23:1-4). The two sisters were Samaria and Jerusalem (representative of Israel and Judah, respectively). They had one mother, that is, these two nations split from the united nation existing from Moses to Solomon. Samaria was named Oholah, meaning "tent woman." This name may have suggested her avocation for religious shrines in contrast to the name for Judah, Oholibah, which means "My tent is in her." This latter title seems to have had direct reference to the Temple (tent, tabernacle) of God which resided in the midst of Jerusalem. Samaria was the eldest or greatest, and Judah was the youngest or smallest (cf. the discussion in chap. 16). Their offspring were their respective inhabitants (cf. v. 10). Both nations were presented as having had immoral sexual relations with Egypt in their youth. The frank descriptions in the passage may bother some, but God was vividly describing the exact character of these peoples. It was there in Egypt, as youths, that these two nations learned to be prostitutes, seeking other nations as lovers, and giving themselves to them (cf. v. 8; Eze 16:26; Jos 24:14; Num 25:3-9; 2 Ki 21:15; Amos 5:25-26).

Samaria's Prostitution (23:5-10). Israel's lovers with whom she played the harlot were the Assyrians and all their impressive and attractively clothed leaders. Israel not only sought political advantages, but also worshiped Assyria's pagan deities (as was customary under Assyrian law).

Israel's judgment was given into the hand of her lover, Assyria, with all her vassals, who uncovered her and executed judgment upon her (the fall of Samaria in 722 B.C.). Samaria became a byword for an immoral nation (similar to the term *Jezebel* and its connotations in our society).

Jerusalem's Prostitution (23:11-35). As in chapter 16, emphasis is given to Jerusalem (Judah), for she was the nation presently under indictment. The passage demonstrates how Jerusalem not only had failed to learn from the perversion of her sister (Israel) and her ultimate judgment, but Judah had acted more wickedly than Samaria in her prostitution of herself to Assyria (cf. Ahaz, 2 Ki 16) and then to the Babylonians (cf. Hezekiah, 2 Ki 20; Jehoahaz and Jehoiakim, 2 Ki 23; and Zedekiah, 2 Ki 24; Jer 29).

Jerusalem's judgment (vv. 22-35) was described as a dismantling of the major organs of her body part by part, perhaps in reference to the deportations of her more important inhabitants in the three deportations (cf. Dan 1:1; 2 Ki 24:10-12, 14-16; 25:11). The remains of the body were consumed by fire and the sword, as would be true in 586 B.C. (cf. 2 Ki 25:18-21). Jerusalem's lovers would take the implements of the Temple, her "jewelry and possessions" (cf. 2 Ki 24:13; 25:13-17). She would be left bare. Her wickedness and fornication would then cease, for with the Babylonian conquest and subsequent captivity, Jerusalem and Judah were left virtually desolate. She would be an harlot no longer. As if Yahweh wanted to make sure that everyone knew why this severe judgment came, He declared the reason in verse 35a: "You [Jerusalem] have forgotten Me [Yahweh] and cast Me behind your back." Judah, therefore, would drink the same cup of His wrath that Samaria drank.

Summary of Chapters 20-23 (23:36-49). This section closed with a summary of the judgments upon Jerusalem and Samaria, and once again the reasons were given: (1) adultery with pagan idols, that is, following after strange gods (v. 37a, forbidden in Ex 22:20; 23:13; Deu 4:15-24; 12:29-32); (2) murder (v. 37b, forbidden in Ex 20:13); (3) the heathen ritual of passing children through a fire in sacrifice (v. 37c, forbidden in Lev 18:21; 20:1-5); (4) defilement of God's sanctuary (v. 38a, forbidden in Ex 20:24-26); (5) profaning of the Sabbaths (v. 38b, forbidden in Ex 20:8-11; Lev 19:3, 30); (6) sacrifice of sons to idols (v. 39; see v. 37c); (7) seeking of security through alliances and political prostitution in which she acquired wealth and ease as she made her lovers drunk (vv. 40-42; cf. Deu 17:14-20 and Eze 20-23).

Therefore, Samaria and Judah would receive the judgment due to an adulteress (v. 47; cf. Deu 22:21-22). Jerusalem was worn out by her prostitution. Her lovers, those with whom she sought alliances, would judge her. She would be cast down, robbed, stoned, killed with the sword, and her houses burned. She would have to bear her sin. But what was the ultimate purpose of the judgment of God: *that Israel shall know that I am Yahweh, the Lord.*

THE ENACTMENT OF JERUSALEM'S JUDGMENT (24:1-27)

SUMMARY

The dreaded yet continually predicted judgment finally had arrived. On the tenth day of the month, December-January, 589/588 (about Dec. 25, 589 B.C.), Nebuchadnezzar commenced the long-prophesied siege of Jerusalem (2 Ki 25:1; Jer 39:1; 52:4). On that same day, God spoke directly to Ezekiel, telling him to announce to the exiles in Babylon that the fateful judgment upon the capital of Judah had begun as predicted. That day would go down in history. It would be a day long remembered by an annual national fast (Zec 8:19).

The Lord had Ezekiel speak a parable in order to portray graphically what was beginning to transpire in Jerusalem. This little poem and its ensuing interpretation describe the judgment of God upon Jerusalem by the Babylonians through the picture of a cooking pot (Jerusalem). This pot would boil its contents (the inhabitants of the city); later the empty pot would burn itself up. This was God's way of cleansing the city, though she did not become completely clean (24:1-14).

How were the exiles to respond to this momentous event? They were to react in the same manner as Ezekiel was to respond, under God's instructions, to the sudden death of his wife: without mourning, crying, or any other normal means of showing grief for the dead. Why? Two reasons are given: (1) With the same lack of natural emotion, the exiles had watched the progressive defilement of the sanctuary of the Lord by the citizens of Jerusalem. (2) This judgment should not have been a surprise to them, for God had foretold this judgment for many years through His prophets. The exiles should have expected it like any other normal event in life (24:15-24).

With the conclusion of these two pictorial representations of the important events of that day, the Lord declared that Ezekiel would now turn and speak directly to the people (24:25-27).

ANNOUNCEMENT OF THE COMMENCEMENT OF THE SIEGE OF JERUSALEM (24:1-2)

As mentioned in the summary above, God directed Ezekiel to announce to the exiles the beginning of the judgment of Jerusalem by Nebuchadnezzar on the very day it started. Thus it was very clear that God was doing what He had promised. He is faithful. The day of dreadful judgment upon Jerusalem and Judah had arrived. The king of Babylon was laying siege to (literally, "resting his weight upon") the city of David.

THE PARABLE OF THE COOKING POT (24:3-14)

In order that the Jews in captivity might understand that the events presently taking place in Jerusalem were really the same judgment that Ezekiel and the other prophets had predicted, God had Ezekiel describe the siege and final judgment upon Jerusalem by means of a parable in verses 3-5. The picture was that of the normal routine of cooking a meal. A cooking pot was placed upon a fire, water was poured into it, the best pieces of meat from the most choice sheep of the flock were placed in the pot and boiled. A pile of bones was placed under the pot for fuel, a common practice.

Verses 6-8 and 9-13 interpreted this parable by identifying some of its elements and by extensions of the figure. The pot was the city of Jerusalem, a city renowned for its killing of innocent people (cf. vv. 2, 6, 9). Though nowhere stated, the contents of the pot would by the analogy represent the inhabitants of Jerusalem. This would mean that the people of Jerusalem are choice people, as indeed they are, being the divinely chosen people of God (cf. Deu 7:6-11). The boiling represented the siege presently being enacted by Babylon.

The contents of the pot—the people—were emphasized in this interpretation. The removal of the contents of the pot, piece by piece, implied that all the inhabitants of Jerusalem would be removed: some—as we know from other prophecies—to death by the sword, and some to captivity. Every one would be affected, both the righteous and the unrighteous. No one would be favored, so to speak, by having a "lot" fall upon him so that he might be delivered from this judgment "by chance."

Another thrust in this interpretation was the exposure of their blood-guiltiness. According to Leviticus 17:13, blood spilt upon the ground had to be covered with dust. Ezekiel picked up this concept and employed it to show that the violent bloodshed of contemporary Jerusalem had not even been covered properly. Jerusalem had not begun to recognize the heinousness of her crimes. Therefore her bloodshed would be thoroughly exposed (in the parable) upon a rock, where all would see it, since the rock would not absorb it. The wrath of God burned against this violence of Jerusalem, as it was doing in the present siege.

Verses 9-13 depict God making the fire hotter under the pot. This was to emphasize the cleansing of Jerusalem. The picture extended the figure by describing the dish being fully cooked until the bones were charred and nothing was left (like our phrase "cooking it to a pulp"). Then the empty pot (the city) was placed upon the fire until it burned, consuming its rust and corruption. The idea is the melting of the pot, resulting in molten metal. Verse 12 declares that the pot (Jerusalem) was resisting this "work" of cleansing. The rust (ASV; identified as wickedness and uncleanness in vv. 11-13) would not completely come off the pot (city). Then the Lord clarified that He had sought to clean Jerusalem through the present judgment upon Jerusalem (not some past disciplines, according to context), but her uncleanness (all the abominations that had stained and corroded her) had not yet been removed. Jerusalem would experience a future cleansing that would be complete.

Yahweh concluded this section with a strong affirmation that this pictorially described judgment was now being enacted. He would not have pity nor change His mind. Jerusalem's own wicked ways were judging her (24:14).

Immediately following this shocking announcement that God was presently judging Jerusalem, Ezekiel received another grim revelation from God: his wife was going to die very soon. This did not seem fair! He had been so faithful to God in his ministry. Why was God compounding Ezekiel's grief at such a time as this?

The answer lies in verse 24. Ezekiel was to be a sign to the exiles. God exhorted Ezekiel in the initial verses of this revelation (vv. 16-17) that he was not to mourn the death of his wife in the normal ways; rather, he would silently grieve and moan quietly. He would not follow the customary funeral practices of removing the shoes and headdress (2 Sa 15:30; Mic 1:8), covering his beard or veiling his face (2 Sa 15:30; 19:5), engaging funeral mourners to wail with sharp repeated cries for the dead (Mic 1:8; 2 Sa 1:17), which was the duty of close relatives (2 Sa 11:26), nor would he eat the "mourning bread" normally brought in sympathy by friends (Jer 16:7). In the morning Ezekiel went about conducting his normal ministry. It was probably at this time that he prophesied his wife's death. That evening his wife died of a plague (v. 18).

The people were stunned at his morning message and its immediate fulfillment. However, the exiles had come to see that Ezekiel's whole life—all he said and did—was a message. Therefore they immediately desired to know the significance of these events (v. 19). The analogy was simple. Just as Ezekiel loved his wife very dearly as the most precious person in his eyes, so the Lord loved His sanctuary in Jerusalem (Ps 132:13-14). The iniquity of Judah had caused God to profane His beloved Temple and Jerusalem through judgment (analagous to the death of Ezekiel's beloved wife) because He is just. Therefore Ezekiel was a picture lesson to the exiles that they were not to mourn over the destruction of the Temple and Jerusalem.

The Temple had become the pride of the Jews (2 Ch 36:19; Lam 1:10-11) and a false source of security (cf. Jer 7:4). The strength of the Lord was supposed to be manifested in the Temple (Ps 43:2; 27:1), but the people had forgotten Yahweh long ago. The Temple structure had become the delight of their eyes and the object of their love. Their boast was of the Temple instead of the living God. But the Temple and the city—as well as the children the exiles had left behind in Jerusalem—were being destroyed. Certainly, of all times, the exiles should have mourned them. Why had God exhorted them not to mourn? Because they should have known that the judgment was coming. It should not have surprised them. They should have expected it. "Do not mourn, Judah! If you and your children had genuinely repented and turned to the Lord and His ways revealed in His word, this would not have happened."

Yahweh loved Jerusalem and the people of God more than Ezekiel loved his wife and the exiles loved their children. Yet, in great agony the Lord had to watch the destruction of His city, His sanctuary, and His people because of His faithfulness to discipline. The exiles would have to bear the burden of their grief silently and pine away because of their iniquities which had brought all this to pass. When the judgment was complete, then they would know that God is the Lord Yahweh. This was both the hope and the purpose of the judgment; it forced people to turn to the Lord when nothing else would.

EZEKIEL'S DUMBNESS WAS TO END (24:25-27)

The previous discussion of the dumbness of Ezekiel in 3:25-27 should be reviewed. When Jerusalem finally fell, and that destruction was subsequently reported to Ezekiel by a fugitive approximately three months later (cf. 2 Ki 25:8; Eze 33:21-22), Ezekiel would no longer be dumb. Then his messages would emphasize hope (Eze 33:21 ff.). Perhaps then the exiles would be ready to listen since his messages of judgment would have been vindicated.

Ezekiel's release from dumbness was to be another dramatic sign to the exiles that God was working through Ezekiel and that all which he proclaimed was true. Through the fulfillment of the judgments of God, spoken and dramatized by Ezekiel (cf. 3:25-27; 24:26-27; 33:21-22), the Jews in Babylon would know that this had been the work of Yahweh, their covenant God.

3

THE SINS OF THE NATIONS AND THEIR RESULTING JUDGMENT

25:1—33:20

THE JUDGMENT UPON THE NATIONS IMMEDIATELY SURROUNDING JUDAH (25:1-17)

SUMMARY

It is customary for expositors of Ezekiel to make a distinct break in the book between chapters 24 and 25, treating chapters 25-32 as a separate and somewhat isolated section of judgment upon the nations. Indeed, judgment upon the nations is the content of these chapters, and in them Ezekiel has gathered together most of the messages of judgment against foreign nations which he received from Yahweh. But at the same time we must also see these chapters in relationship to the overall context and development of the book, especially to the immediate context of chapter 24.

Chapter 24 begins with a specific date, the date of the beginning of the fall of Jerusalem to Babylon, and proceeds to discuss that judgment. Chapter 25 is a continuation of that judgment message of Ezekiel. Nothing warrants a *major* break between chapters 24 and 25 any more than there should be a break between the parable of the pot in 24:3-14 and Ezekiel's role as a sign to the exiles in 24:15-24.

Chapters 24 and 25 logically form a single message. The Lord had just announced the commencement of his long-prophesied judgment upon Jerusalem and Judah. From the prophecy in chapter 25 we see that the nations immediately surrounding Judah (Ammon, Moab, Edom, and Philistia) appeared to be sitting on the sidelines cheering at the destruction of Jerusalem and Judah, hoping for some spoils for themselves. Lest this gleeful taunting continue and the exiles question the promises of God, the Lord immediately announced judgment upon these nations.

This announcement of judgment should not have come as a surprise upon these nations any more than Judah's judgment should have startled her. Several times Jeremiah, the prophet, had prophesied judgment upon these nations (cf. Jer 25:1-26; 9:26; 27:1-11; 47:1-7; 48:1-47; 49:1-22). They too would endure the seventy years of captivity in Babylon (Jer 25:11) enacted by Nebuchadnezzar.

Had not God promised to Abraham in the Abrahamic covenant that the one who cursed Israel would likewise be cursed (Gen 12:3)? Each of these four nations had mistreated Israel and disdained her, especially at this time of her discipline. God was as faithful to exact His punishment upon these nations in keeping with His covenant to Abraham as He was faithful to punish Judah according to His covenant, the Mosaic covenant, with her.

The judgment of the nations would begin with the invasion of Babylon and continue until the end times when Judah will possess these nations and the Lord will reign (cf. Is 11:14; Dan 11:41; Joel 3:1-4). Their judgment is viewed as one single judgment which began with Nebuchadnezzar and will conclude with the second coming of Christ. The judgment is looked upon as a unit, not as several different judgments.

The result of the Lord's judgment upon Ammon, Moab, Edom, and Philistia was to be the same as that for Judah. It was to bring these nations to the ultimate realization that Yahweh was who He said He was: the only God. As with Judah, judgment seemed to be the only way these nations could be made to understand this truth.

The prophecy against each nation contained three essential elements: the reason for the judgment, the description of the judgment, and the result of the judgment. These three parts of each prophecy are treated here.

PROPHECY AGAINST AMMON (25:1-7)

Ammon would be judged because she rejoiced with contempt, clap-

81

ping her hands and stomping her feet at the profaning of the Temple, the desolation of the land, and the exile of Judah (vv. 3b, 6; cf. Zep 2:8, 10). When Nebuchadnezzar chose to deal with Jerusalem before Ammon (cf. 21:20, 28-32), Ammon must have begun to rejoice over the pillage of Jerusalem and the fall of Judah.

The Lord declared that her judgment (vv. 4-5, 7) would be executed by the "children of the east" (ASV). This latter phrase is employed throughout the Scriptures in reference to any people to the east of another people, but never is it stereotyped as meaning only one specific nation. In the light of Jeremiah 25:11, 19-20; 27:1-11; 40:11-14; 41: 10, 15; and 49:3-5, it seems certain that Nebuchadnezzar executed this judgment shortly after the fall of Jerusalem. Josephus (*Antiquities* 10. 9. 7) also records that Nebuchadnezzar brought Ammon and Moab into subjection in the fifth year after the fall of Jerusalem (*c.* 582/1 B.C.). Ezekiel declared that Ammon would be exploited by its conqueror, and Ammon's capital, Rabbath Ammon, would be left desolate and would be of no use except as a stable for camels and a shearing floor. The Ammonite nation would lie in ruins until the end times when that nation will be restored (Jer 49:6), though possessed by Judah (Is 11:14).

The result of this judgment would be that Ammon would know that the Lord truly is Yahweh (Eze 25:7).

PROPHECY AGAINST MOAB (25:8-11)

Moab lacked respect for Judah and her divine election. God called Judah to be an instrument of blessing as His own people, but Moab laughed at Judah (Jer 48:27; Zep 2:8-9) and likened her to all the other nations (v. 8). Because Moab so degraded Judah, she too would be punished.

The judgment of Moab was closely associated with that of Ammon, as had been true throughout her history (Gen 19:37-38). When Babylon would execute Yahweh's judgment upon the children of Ammon, Yahweh would also deliver Moab to these "children of the East." This is in keeping with Josephus's record that Nebuchadnezzar subjugated both Ammon and Moab in 582/1 B.C. Moab's northwest flank ("shoulder") would be exposed to the invaders along the line of Beth-jeshimoth to Baal-meon toward Kirjath-Arim. Jeremiah declared that Moab would be exiled and laid desolate (Jer 48:7-9). Along with Ammon, Moab would be remembered no more among the nations until the end times (v. 10; Is 11:14).

The result of this judgment would be the same as that for Ammon: Moab would come to know that the true Lord is Yahweh, the God of Israel.

PROPHECY AGAINST EDOM (25:12-14)

Vengeance had continually characterized Edom's attitude toward Judah. From the beginning of that nation, centered in the conflict between Esau and Jacob over the birthright and blessing, Edom (named for Esau) had been at enmity with Judah (cf. Num 20:14-23; 1 Ki 11:14; 2 Ch 28:17; Amos 1:11-12). Edom, along with Moab and Ammon, degraded Judah and laughed at the idea of her destruction (cf. v. 8; Lam 4:21-22; Ps 137:1, 7-9; Eze 36:5).

Because of this attitude toward Judah, the Lord would take vengeance upon Edom in judgment (v. 14). He would make Edom desolate throughout her territory from Teman to Dedan (v. 13). Though no specific instrument of judgment is mentioned in this passage, Jeremiah 49:10, 14; 9:26; 25:21; and 27:1-11 imply that Edom was judged along with the nations around her at the time of Nebuchadnezzar. Ezekiel 32:29 represents Edom as slain prior to the fall of Egypt, and Malachi 1:2-5 depicts Edom's judgment as past. However, though Edom apparently was judged by Nebuchadnezzar, verse 14 states that the Lord's vengeance would also be executed by the hand of Judah. Certainly Judah, destroyed and taken captive by Babylon, did not execute judgment upon Edom immediately after her fall, nor is there any record that she ever did. This reference undoubtedly pertains to the future end times when Isaiah 11:14 and Amos 9:12 declare that Israel shall possess Edom at the time of the Messiah's reign (cf. Eze 35; Ob 18; Dan 11:41). Therefore the judgment upon these nations obviously encompasses a long period of time: from Nebuchadnezzar's invasion (a near judgment) to the second coming of Christ (a future judgment).

The result of Edom's judgment was slightly different from those above. Verse 14b states that Edom would know the Lord's vengeance. One would also have to say that at that time they too shall know that He is the true God.

PROPHECY AGAINST PHILISTIA (25:15-16)

The Philistines, who traditionally inhabited the southern coastal plain of Judah, were depicted as those who had acted with contemptuous and perpetual vengeance and enmity against Judah. This can be observed during the times of Samson (Judg 13), Eli (1 Sa 4), Saul (1 Sa 13;31), David (2 Sa 5), Hezekiah (2 Ki 18), Jehoram (2 Ch 21), and Ahaz (2 Ch 28).

Because of Philistia's continual desire to destroy Judah, God, in faithfulness to the Abrahamic covenant (cf. Gen 12:3), would execute His vengeance upon this nation, but in the sense of discipline for correction. He would cut off the Cherethites (another name for the Philistines as well as for a specific group of them). Though no time nor instrument of judgment is declared in this passage, in keeping with the context and parallel passages, it may be concluded that Philistia's judgment was similar to the other three nations previously mentioned. Her discipline began with Nebuchadnezzar's invasion (cf. Jer 25:20; 47:1-7) and will be ultimately concluded with Israel's possession of Philistia at the end times when Yahweh will restore the fortunes of Judah (cf. Is 11:14; Joel 3:1-4; Ob 19; Zep 2:4-7).

The result of Philistia's judgment is like that of the other nations discussed: she will know through this judgment that the true God is Yahweh, the God of Israel.

THE JUDGMENT UPON TYRE AND SIDON
(26:1—28:26)

SUMMARY

It is interesting in Scripture to note that the cities of Tyre and Sidon are normally linked together in whatever the discussion may be. Tyre was the leader of the two for most of the first millennium B.C., and is therefore the prominent city in this message of Ezekiel.

Historical records concerning Tyre and Sidon are relatively sparse. However, enough evidence can be scraped together to form a skeleton history of Tyre. From the time of Solomon, Tyre, a prominent city of

Phoenicia, had been known both for its sea trade and merchant activity on land. Tyre was looked upon as the queen of the sea merchants, being politically strong and gaining much wealth and prosperity from her trade. The city was divided into two parts: the mainland section and the island. The walled city on the island provided an almost impregnable fortress in times of war. Tyre had submitted to the sovereignty of Assyria; but with the decline of the Assyrian state, Tyre had become independent and politically and commercially strong. It was against this strong city that Ezekiel announced the forthcoming judgment.

Three chapters in this judgment section against foreign nations pertain to the city of Tyre. Why is this unproportionate amount of space given to a city? The answer lies both in the prominence of Tyre and in the reason for her judgment.

A typical judgment oracle of the prophets is found in 26:1-14. The accusation by Yahweh was made against Tyre, followed by the verdict of judgment by the great Judge, Yahweh. Tyre had sought to take advantage of Jerusalem when that city turned to her for help in the midst of the Babylonian siege of Jerusalem. Tyre looked upon that event as an opportunity for her to acquire her "fill" of the spoils of Jerusalem (v. 2). For this cause, Yahweh announced that many nations (especially Babylon) would receive their fill of the spoils of Tyre and would roll over her in succession as waves of the sea. The ultimate end would be the desolation of Tyre as a bare, smooth, seaworn rock, a city never again to be rebuilt. Once more the major purpose of Yahweh's judgment was set forth: Tyre would know that the Lord is Yahweh through His judgment upon her (v. 6).

The reaction of the nations who had been dependent upon Tyre and worked for her was one of surprise and fear at her destruction (26:15-18). How could mighty Tyre fall? The leaders of these satellites sang a dirge over Tyre, summarizing her fall and the results thereof.

In chapter 27 Ezekiel was encouraged by Yahweh to lift up a dirge over Tyre. Such a dirge was sung (encompassing the entire chapter) in which Ezekiel likened Tyre to a proud and beautiful ship constructed with materials transported by her sea merchants from all over the ancient Near East. She subjugated peoples to work for her as oarsmen, maintenance personnel, and traders. The ship (the empire of Tyre) became more and more wealthy, prominent, and prosperous, entering commercial relations with most countries of that day and securing wares of every kind. Finally, however, the ship became so heavily laden with its luxurious prosperity that it was portrayed as sinking under the strong east wind (Babylon), an event which raised the mournful laments of all those working on or for this ship of Tyre.

Ezekiel concluded this judgment against Tyre (chap. 28) by indicting the ruler of Tyre for thinking that he was God. The reason for this self-exaltation was the working of Satan in and through (if not indwelling) him. When the prince would be destroyed in death, then it would be vividly clear that he was only a man.

THE JUDGMENT ORACLE AGAINST TYRE (26:1-14)

The two aspects of this judgment oracle are the accusation (reason for judgment) in verse 2 and the verdict (announced judgment) in verses 3 to 14. Jerusalem found herself in the midst of a siege by Babylon and appeared to be turning to Tyre for aid. Tyre was accused of desiring to fill herself with the spoils of Jerusalem by taking advantage of Jerusalem's predicament.

Yahweh did not even wait until after the destruction of Jerusalem (c. Nov., 586 B.C.) to announce judgment upon Tyre, but He predicted the siege and spoil of Tyre by Babylon and other nations while Jerusalem was still under siege in 587 B.C. Since the month of the year is not stated in verse 1, it is impossible to be more specific regarding this date.

A general statement of judgment is set forth in verses 3-6. Many nations would be employed by Yahweh to bring judgment upon Tyre. They would come in succession as the waves of the sea (v. 3). History supports this prediction, for Babylon, Persia, Greece, the Ptolemies, the Seleucids, and Rome all had dominion over Tyre. Today the ancient city of Tyre lies in ruins, essentially the ruins of the Roman period. This agrees with the total desolation of Tyre proclaimed in verses 4 and 5. Tyre was to become like a bare, smooth, sea-washed rock fit only for the drying of fishing nets. Because she desired to spoil Jerusalem, she would become the spoil of nations (note the plural).

Though verses 7 through 14 specify the immediate judgment by Nebuchadnezzar (probably following the fall of Jerusalem), the plural forms of the word "nation" in verses 3 and 5 show that this judgment was not confined to Babylon alone. Verses 12-14 change the pronoun from "he" (reference to Nebuchadnezzar) to "they" (reference to the many nations) who would judge Tyre. Verses 7-11 detail the thirteen-year siege that Nebuchadnezzar brought against Tyre (cf. Josephus's *Antiqquities* 10. 9. 1), agreeing with the general conquest of this whole area by Nebuchadnezzar as prophesied not only in Ezekiel, but also in Isaiah 23:1-18 and Jeremiah 25:22-26; 27:3-8; and 47:4-7. Tyre would never be built again (v. 14). Today ancient Tyre lies in this state of predicted ruins.

Yahweh's compassion in judgment was demonstrated in His basic purpose for this judgment upon Tyre: "and they shall know that I am the LORD [Yahweh]" (26:6).

THE REACTION OF OTHERS TO THE FALL OF TYRE (26:15-18)

The many vassal cities (and their leaders) under the dominion of Tyre were stunned by her downfall. How could the great Tyre collapse? Trembling and dismayed, they responded with a funeral dirge over Tyre.

YAHWEH'S VERDICT (26:19-21)

Yahweh summarized the verdict of verses 3-6, reminding Tyre that she would never reign again. She would die and not experience the honor of those who live in "the land of the living."

EZEKIEL'S DIRGE OVER TYRE (27:1-36)

This song, sung by Ezekiel, portrays Tyre as a glorious ship built through commercial prowess. But this marvelous ship ultimately sinks under the combined effect of the weight of her laden wares which she had acquired and the strong east wind (Babylon). The emphasis of the dirge demonstrates that Tyre's whole purpose for existence has been the acquisition of wealth and prosperity. When such a goal obsesses a people, the ultimate result is collapse. Tyre is a vivid reminder to all that riches are not the goal and purpose of life. The main purpose of life is to know that the Lord is our God (cf. Eze 26:6).

JUDGMENT UPON THE RULER OF TYRE (28:1-19)

Various approaches have been taken to this difficult section of Ezekiel. Some have resorted to ancient mythology to explain this passage. Others simply alter the text to say what they think it should say.

There is no basis in this passage, nor in normal principles of interpretation, for seeking to introduce ancient mythology as the explanation of these verses. Nor are there any grounds for changing the text. A normal interpretive approach, with its understanding of figurative language, satisfactorily explains the passage. The context argues that the message in verses 1-10 and the message in verses 11-19 both spoke about the same ruler of Tyre. The words "prince" and "king" are often used interchangeably in the Old Testament (cf. 1 Sa 9:16; 10:1; 15:17; 2 Sa 7:8) for the ruler of a people. There is no reason to assume that two different people are meant. On the other hand, the common phrase "the word of the LORD [Yahweh] came unto me, saying" is employed both in verse 1 and in verse 11 to indicate two distinct messages about the judgment of the ruler of Tyre: the first describing his indictment and judgment; the second portraying the real individual (or spirit) who was behind the actions and thoughts of the king of Tyre: Satan.

The message in verses 1-10 was a judgment message against the prince of Tyre. The accusation (reason for judgment) is set forth in verses 2-5. This prince inwardly exalted himself as God and outwardly declared himself to be God. He was proud of his accumulated riches acquired through his wisdom. But, because of his self-exaltation as God, he would be judged. In verses 2b-3, Yahweh rebuked this ruler for his claim to deity, reminding the prince that he was only a man.

Yahweh's verdict (vv. 6-10) states that He would bring foreigners upon the ruler of Tyre (cf. 26:2-6). They would destroy his splendor and wisdom, putting him to death. The death of Tyre's ruler would demonstrate that he is not God.

The second message, in verses 11-19, was Ezekiel's dirge over the king of Tyre in which he described the king as controlled by Satan. Through comparison with the account of man's Fall in Genesis 3, this passage is understood to portray Satan as the one who was behind the actions, thoughts, and motives of the king of Tyre. This king was simply a tool of Satan, probably indwelt by Satan.

The description in verses 12-17 fits only Satan, though in this case Satan was indwelling a man: the king of Tyre. He was a "seal of perfection," filled with wisdom, entirely beautiful and covered with precious stones. He was in the Garden of Eden (cf. Gen 3) and was an anointed covering cherub (in the sense of a "guardian"; cf. 1 Ki 8:7; 1 Ch 28:18; Ex 25:20; 37:9) on the holy mountain of God. He was perfect in his ways from his creation. Yet he sinned (vv. 15-18) and was cast to the earth, and his position as a guardian cherub was destroyed. Satan and the human king of Tyre whom he indwelt (cf. 28:6-10) would be devoured (vv. 18-19).

JUDGMENT ORACLE ON SIDON (28:20-24)

This judgment on Sidon is extremely brief, almost like an appendage to the previous judgment message upon Tyre. This is probably due to the inferior relationship of Sidon to Tyre. Sidon followed the "footsteps" of Tyre. Sidon's judgment will be bloodshed and pestilence. In this judgment Yahweh would be honored in that Sidon would come to know that He is Yahweh.

Verse 24 summarizes the preceding oracles of judgment. Israel would be free from those nations who pricked her like a briar when the judgments of Yahweh would be completed. When Israel observed these judgments upon Tyre and Sidon, then she also would know that Yahweh is her God.

PROMISE OF RESTORATION FOR THE HOUSE OF ISRAEL (28:25-26)

The security and prosperity of Israel in the land of Palestine following her future restoration to that land by Yahweh is described in these verses, demonstrating that then Israel would know that "I am Yahweh their God."

THE JUDGMENT UPON EGYPT (29:1—33:20)

SUMMARY

In order to understand the judgment upon Egypt related in these chapters, it is necessary to outline the basic history of Ezekiel's day. The following outline will give a necessary frame of reference for the study of the ensuing chapters:

597 B.C.: The captivity of Jehoiachin and others from Jerusalem by the Babylonians occurred (2 Ki 24:12). The beginning of Zedekiah's regency followed shortly (2 Ki 24:18).

December/January, 589/88 B.C.: The Babylonian siege of Jerusalem began (2 Ki 25:1; Eze 24:1-2).

588 B.C.: Sometime during this year, Hophra (Apries), the king of Egypt, interrupted the Babylonian siege of Jerusalem by sending an Egyptian task force to aid Judah (Jer 37:5-11). Apparently there existed a defense agreement between Zedekiah and Hophra by which Hophra would send aid in the event of an attack upon Judah.

December/January, 588/87 B.C.: Ezekiel prophesied judgment against Pharaoh and Egypt, undoubtedly precipitated by Hophra's intervention (Eze 29:1-16).

March/April, 587 B.C.: Ezekiel described the initial defeat of Pharaoh Hophra and then predicted the complete desolation of Egypt at the hands of the Babylonians (Eze 30:20-26).

May/June, 587 B.C.: Ezekiel prophesied a complete desolation of Egypt, emphasizing her pride as the cause (Eze 31:1-18).

September/November, 587 B.C.: Jeremiah described the siege of Jerusalem as still in process (Jer 32:1-5).

August, 586 B.C.: Zedekiah's regency was terminated (2 Ki 25:8).

September, 586 B.C.: The siege of Jerusalem and its destruction were completed (2 Ki 25:8).

December, 586 B.C.: The report of Jerusalem's fall reached the exiles in Babylon (Eze 33:21).

March, 585 B.C.: Ezekiel sang a funeral dirge for Pharaoh (Eze 32:1-16).

April, 585 B.C.: Ezekiel lamented the fall of Pharaoh and Egypt and then gave a final warning to the Jews both in Judah and also in the exile to turn from their iniquities to Yahweh (Eze 32:17—33:20).

There is a chronological and historical orientation to Ezekiel's prophecies. This book progresses from the reasons for the coming judgment upon Judah and Jerusalem, to the announcement of the beginning of that judgment, followed by what God will do with those nations who mistreat Judah. The fall of Jerusalem is pivotal in the development of the book. The announcement and description of Judah's judgment, and the judgment upon those nations who have cursed Israel in violation of the Abrahamic covenant, precede the fall of Jerusalem, while the announcement of future hope and restoration follows that event. One must respect and adhere to the chronological notices which Ezekiel constantly inserts at the beginning of each message group in order to understand the logical development of his theme.

A review of the development of Ezekiel's argument up to this point is needed. Chapter 24 discusses the commencement of the long-prophesied judgment upon Israel by describing the siege of Jerusalem by Babylon. Chapter 25 follows with the announcement of judgment upon the nations immediately surrounding Judah (Ammon, Moab, Edom, and Philistia) because they were cheering the destruction of Jerusalem and hoping for spoils. God announced judgment upon them in keeping with the Abrahamic covenant (Gen 12:3). Chapters 26-28 set forth a similar judgment upon the haughty king of Tyre (and his city) who sought to take advantage of Jerusalem in the midst of her siege in order to gain riches for himself. Now chapters 29-32 will spell out judgment upon Egypt because of her pride and failure to support Israel when she needed help.

The literary structure of this judgment oracle upon Egypt will now be outlined. A general prophecy of judgment against Pharaoh and Egypt is proclaimed in 29:1-16 (probably precipitated by the Egyptian invasion described in Jer 37:5-8). The next message (in 29:17—30: 19) is dated 571 B.C., the last dated message in the book of Ezekiel. Though it might seem to be out of place in light of Ezekiel's chronological arrangement, it really is not. Rather, Ezekiel's organization of the messages of his prophecy places this later prophecy here in order to provide a logical sequence in the announcement of judgment upon Egypt by showing (1) the relation of Egypt to Tyre and (2) the time when the full judgment upon Egypt would be enacted. The understanding of this "time" sheds light upon a proper understanding of 30:20-26 and the following messages.

There are four additional messages of judgment upon Egypt. The first (30:20-26) describes the initial defeat of Pharaoh Hophra in 588 B.C. and then proceeds to announce a more complete and final defeat of Egypt (as described in 29:17—30:19). Chapter 31 highlights the root cause in Egypt's nature that has brought about the wrath of Yahweh: pride. This is beautifully illustrated by likening Egypt to Assyria (Asshur) which is portrayed as a great cedar of Lebanon, finer than any other tree. Ezekiel reminds Egypt that she will be cut down just as Yahweh cut down Assyria. Egypt should have learned from Yahweh's judgment upon Assyria, but she did not. After the fall of Jerusalem, Ezekiel sings the funeral dirge over Pharaoh and Egypt, summarizing the details of God's punishment and demonstrating the certainty and finality of her destruction. Egypt will go down to the pit: to Sheol (Eze 32:1-16).

The last oracle in Ezekiel 32:17—33:20 encompasses two messages given on the same day. The first (32:17-32) gives a concluding summary of Egypt's judgment by means of a lament by Ezekiel. Egypt will go down to the pit like all uncircumcised nations who were "the terror of the mighty in the land of the living" (v. 27). In other words, they have been violent in their dealings with other human beings and nations in this life. Now Yahweh has set His terror in the land of the living (v. 32) against Egypt. In case the Jews might begin to rejoice over the announced judgments upon these other nations and miss the thrust of Ezekiel 1-24, Yahweh reminded them of Ezekiel's role as a watchman. The Lord, through this message (33:1-20), exhorted the people of Israel to take advantage of the present opportunity to turn from their individual iniquities and live. Jerusalem would fall, but individuals can always live. It was time to repent!

Each portion of the prophecy against Egypt will be discussed with respect to its essential messages of judgment, the reason for that judgment, the purpose of God in the judgment, and major problems that may arise.

The basic prophecy against Pharaoh and all Egypt (29:1-16)

Pharaoh is likened to a sea monster, and his satellite nations to fish that cling to him. He will be hooked by Yahweh and cast upon the wilderness field to be devoured by birds and animals (29:2-5). This vivid description of Egypt's judgment was announced by Ezekiel on the twelfth day of December/January, 588/87 B.C. (29:1), one full year after the beginning of the siege of Jerusalem by Nebuchadnezzar.

Pharaoh Hophra's interruption of the siege of Jerusalem in 588 B.C. undoubtedly gave rise to this judgment. The Greek historian Herodotus also implies that Pharaoh Apries (Hophra) was so strong in his position that he felt no god could dislodge him. This is consistent with one of the basic reasons why Yahweh brought this judgment upon Egypt: Pharaoh's pride in looking upon himself as the creator of the Nile (29:9c). However, the judgment was not limited to Hophra. The other cause for this judgment resided in Egypt's failure throughout her history to be a support of Israel (29:6b-7). On the contrary, Egypt always performed like a broken reed when Israel sought to lean upon her, just as in this present failure of Hophra. The people of Egypt would be scattered among the nations for forty years (29:10-12; cf. 30:23) and the land of Egypt would lie desolate from Migdol, one of the northernmost cities, to Syene (at Aswan), at the southern border of Egypt. In other words, all of Egypt would lie waste with its inhabitants scattered among the nations for forty years.

A problem with this prophecy is the lack of any extrabiblical historical reference to this forty-year period in Egyptian history. The sources for Egyptian history during this period are scarce, and most information comes from Herodotus. He drew upon secondary sources, and it has been demonstrated that his historial data at times can be faulty. Also the kings of the ancient Near East seldom admitted or recounted their defeats. To expect to find records of such a judgment upon Egypt as described above would be most unlikely. Likewise, Babylonian records are sparse for this period. Therefore, it must be concluded that Ezekiel was recounting a destruction of Egypt for forty years which was not necessarily seen in the sparse extrabiblical data, but the judgment was nevertheless accurate.

Babylonian records do imply that Nebuchadnezzar invaded Egypt shortly after 570 B.C. (cf. 29:17—30:19), while Berossus, the historian of Babylon, declares that Nebuchadnezzar did take great numbers of Egyptians captive to Babylon after he conquered Egypt. Both of these factors are in harmony with the prophecy of Ezekiel in this section.

The foundational principle and purpose in Yahweh's judgments was again the purpose for His judgment upon Egypt. Through this judgment all the inhabitants of Egypt *would know that He is Yahweh* (29: 6a, 9b).

Then Ezekiel announced an interesting addition to this judgment upon Egypt, one not often found in judgment oracles against foreign nations: Egypt would be restored to the land of Egypt after the forty-year period. This restoration may have paralleled the rise of Persia and her more lenient policy (in contrast to Babylon) toward the nations (29:13-16). Verse 14 is strategic for understanding this whole prophecy, for it emphasizes that "captives" were taken to Babylon (with which Berossus agrees) and they would be returned to Pathros, the upper, or southern portion of Egypt. Yet this verse quickly asserts that Egypt would never rule again among the nations after this restoration, but would be a lowly nation. Such has been her lot in history.

THE DETAIL JUDGMENT UPON EGYPT AND ITS RELATION TO TYRE (29:17—30:19)

One of the more perplexing problems in the judgment oracles against Egypt is the date of this section. March/April, 571 B.C. makes this the latest dated message in this entire book. If Ezekiel was basically following a chronological approach to the organization of his prophecy, why did he insert this message here?

Several answers may be given. First, the placement of this prophecy at this point in the book provides an important transition between the judgments upon Tyre and upon Egypt. It helps explain why Tyre is so important in Ezekiel's prophecy. Though the prophecy of this judgment upon Egypt was not received until after the subjugation of Tyre by Nebuchadnezzar, it is inserted here with the rest of the oracles against Egypt in order to provide a logical comparison between the fall of Tyre and the coming judgment upon Egypt. A comparison between the sparse spoils of Tyre received by Babylon and Babylon's hope of booty from Egypt could not have been made before 571 B.C. and could not have had much meaning for the Egyptians. However, after 571 B.C., Egypt would know of the long, hard, thirteen-year siege of Tyre and how Babylon received practically no spoils due to the maritime aid of Egypt to Tyre which enabled Tyre to send away her wealth during the siege of that city, so that the Babylonians received nothing when they entered the city.

Second, this message belongs in this place topically and logically. Though Ezekiel was not arranging his prophecy solely on a topical basis, he did logically arrange this group of judgments against Egypt. This message belongs after the introductory judgment oracle in 29:1-16 in order to show when the full enactment of the predicted judgment would occur.

Had this message not been inserted at this point, the following messages in the oracles against Egypt may have been misunderstood by the readers of Ezekiel's prophecy. Thus this message must precede those following in order to give the full scope of the judgment before a partial judgment concept is introduced. Ezekiel 30:20-26 begins with a statement of the initial judgment upon Pharaoh Hophra (Apries) and then continues to discuss the more complete judgment which was to occur after 571 B.C. If the full scope of the 571 B.C. message had not been inserted here, one might have taken the descriptions of judgment in chapter 31 and the dirge in chapter 32 to refer only to initial judgment upon Hophra and not in reference to the full judgment upon Egypt. Though the messages of 30:20 and following are delivered before that of 29:17—30:19, according to their dates, the insertion of the 571 B.C. oracle at this point in the arrangement of messages is necessary to give a proper understanding to those who would read Ezekiel's prophecy.

There are two aspects of this dated message of 571 B.C. The relation of Egypt's judgment to that of Tyre is described in 29:17-21. Looking upon the siege and subjugation of Tyre as a past event, Ezekiel related how Nebuchadnezzar and his army labored hard against Tyre for thirteen years (cf. Josephus's *Antiquities* 10. 11. 1). From the scraps of historical data available, it appears that Egypt and Tyre had become allies under Hophra (Apries). The prolonged siege of Tyre by Babylon was perhaps due to the aid of the Egyptians. This would explain why Yahweh declared that He would give the spoils of the land of Egypt to Nebuchadnezzar in place of the lack of such spoils at Tyre due to the intervention, in part, of Egypt on the behalf of Tyre. Because Egypt had opposed Yahweh's purposes by aiding Tyre (29:20*b*), the Babylonians would receive commensurate wages for the labor they would expend during the coming invasion of Egypt (29:17-21).

On the day that Egypt was conquered by Nebuchadnezzar and the forty years of captivity began, two things were to occur with respect to the exiles of Israel in Babylon: (1) They would be encouraged and strengthened concerning God's faithfulness and work, and (2) Ezekiel would be given freedom of speech in their midst. The phrase "cause a horn to [sprout] to . . . Israel" (v. 21, ASV) is perhaps unclear. A "horn" is used throughout the Old Testament to figuratively represent essentially two concepts: (1) strength, and (2) a leader or ruler. Some compare the phrase in this passage to that in Psalm 132:17 and declare that it refers to the Messiah. Yet the context seems to mitigate against this position. This whole section of judgment upon Egypt is historically related; and, in fact, verse 21 explicitly declares that the horn will sprout in the day of Babylon's completion of the judgment upon Egypt. Certainly no Messiah comes upon the scene at that time. Therefore, it seems best to understand the phrase as a statement that Israel (in exile) would be "strengthened" or "encouraged" by the destruction of Egypt (her long-time enemy) in harmony with the promises of cursing in the Abrahamic covenant (Gen 12:3). In addition, Ezekiel would be given an open mouth to proclaim and discuss God's purpose among the exiles more freely when they observed the fulfillment of his predictions upon Egypt. They would realize that he was truly a spokesman for God.

The purpose of this judgment has its normal thrust, this time with respect to Israel. Through the judgment of Yahweh upon Egypt, Israel would recognize that He is Yahweh, the One who is faithful to His covenants and promises.

The second aspect of this dated oracle (30:1-19) emphasizes the imminency of the Babylonian judgment upon Egypt. Some expositors have seen a reference to the future end times in the beginning phrases of this secton. In the prophetic books, the phrases "the day of Yahweh" and "a day of cloud" normally refer to the "Day of the Lord" at the end of history. However, several factors argue against such an understanding of the phrases in this context. First, the specific reference in the context is to Egypt and her satellites alone. Jews living in Egypt are the "children of the land of covenant," having fled Palestine with the murder of Gedaliah (cf. 2 Ki 25:23-26). They will be judged along with Egypt. Second, the invaders take the spoils of Egypt, just as has been delineated in the previous section (29:17-21). Third, the area taken is the same as that described in Ezekiel 29:10, "from Migdol to Syene" (see 30:6, NASB). Fourth, the event is called the "day of Egypt" in verse 9, seeming to limit the judgment to Egypt. Fifth, Nebuchadnezzar is explicitly stated to be the one who will stop the multitude of Egypt (30:10) and cause idolatry to perish (30:13). Sixth, specific judgment is prophesied upon the present cities of Egypt as they were known in Ezekiel's day (30:14-18). Seventh, the "time of nations" (30:3, ASV) correlates with Ezekiel 25-32, where this period is described as a time in which Babylon executes judgment upon the nations (cf. Jer 25, 27, 45-49). Last, there will be a captivity of the young men and the "daughters" (maybe in reference to her satellites), a captivity described with the same phrase as verse 3: a "cloud" upon Egypt (Eze 30:18). The combined weight of this context argues strongly for the "day of the LORD" (v. 3) in this context to refer to the judgment of Yahweh upon Egypt through Nebuchadnezzar, rather than the judgment of Yahweh upon Egypt at the end times. Context is more important as an interpretive principle than the stereotyping of a phrase or symbol.

Therefore, the second aspect of the message declares the nearness of the judgment and details its enactment (as seen in the above paragraph). Babylonian records indicate an invasion of Egypt by Nebuchadnezzar around 568 B.C. Such an invasion would be three years after the issuance of this prophecy. Though both Babylonian and Egyptian records do not clearly mention such an invasion and captivity (as discussed above), one can be confident that such judgment did occur on the basis of this word from God.

When this judgment is enacted by Babylon upon Egypt, the fruition of Yahweh's judgment will be accomplished: Egypt will know that the true God is Yahweh (30:8, 19).

EGYPT'S PARTIAL AND COMPLETE DEFEAT BY NEBUCHADNEZZAR
 (30:20-26)

This short message was delivered in March/April, 587 B.C., about three months after the oracle of 29:1-16. The familiar symbol of "the arm of Pharaoh," flexed, and wielding a sword in battle, was employed by Ezekiel to stress the might and power of the king. Hophra (Apries) took as his title the Egyptian phrase meaning "possessed of a muscular arm—a strong-armed man." Ezekiel captured the imagery of this title to describe the defeat of Hophra when he intervened in Palestine in 588 B.C.; Yahweh shattered Hophra's arm or strength (30:21). This partial defeat occurred in 588 B.C. before this message was delivered.

Ezekiel went on to declare that both arms of Pharaoh would be shattered, the strong one and the one already shattered in 588 B.C. which never healed (30:22). The image of a god giving his sword to a pharaoh is another popular symbol in Egyptian literature and sculpture to depict the source of a king's strength. Ironically, the complete defeat of Egypt would be accomplished when Yahweh, the true God, places His sword in the hand of Nebuchadnezzar, the king of Babylon, to "strengthen" him to crush the "arms" (the strength) of the pharaoh. This future thorough conquest of Egypt is the judgment which is predicted in the message of 29:17—30:19. As a result of this defeat, the Egyptians would be scattered among the nations (30:23, 26a; cf. 29: 12; 30:17-18).

The purpose of Yahweh's judgment was always stressed by Ezekiel, for he did not want anyone to misunderstand the goal of Yahweh's judgment. God's judgments are to bring people to the knowledge of God. This judgment would cause Egypt to know that the Lord is Yahweh (30: 25-26).

EGYPT'S DOWNFALL COMPARED TO ASSYRIA'S COLLAPSE (31:1-18)

On the first day of May/June, 587 B.C., two months after the preceding message, Ezekiel pointed out the central fault of Egypt and her pharaohs: pride. Egypt had always boasted in her greatness (v. 10). In order to cause Egypt to see the nature of her pride, Ezekiel likened Egypt to the great, proud, and powerful nation of Assyria which ruled the ancient Near East from approximately 860 to 612 B.C. (31:2). Assyria is portrayed as a great cedar of Lebanon, in fact, a tree that was envied by all other trees (nations) that were planted in the world and in the Garden of Eden. It was "higher" than other trees (nations), provided shade and water for all nations, and had beautiful and long branches (31:3-9). This imagery illustrates Assyria's pride over her world status.

In like manner to Assyria, Pharaoh had let his heart rise high in pride. However, Yahweh was about to cut down Egypt just as He chopped down the "great tree" of Assyria (31:10-14). Yahweh would give Egypt into the hand of the "mighty one" of the nations. The term "mighty one" is employed in the Old Testament in reference to a chief man or a leader (cf. 2 Ki 24:15; Eze 17:13). From the context of this passage, it seems most certain that Nebuchadnezzar, the chief ruler of the nations of his day, was the instrument that God would use to humble Egypt.

Egypt would die. She would go down to Sheol, the place of the dead, where other nations (trees) have descended. Though great like Assyria, Egypt could not escape the death that was common to ordinary nations (trees). Her death and burial would be barbarous like that of the uncircumcised. This would be humiliating, for Egyptians normally practiced circumcision and meticulous burial practices (31:16-18).

Egypt should have learned from the downfall of Assyria, but she did not. Yahweh is saddened when nations go contrary to His ways and must receive judgment. As a result, the Lord mourned over Egypt's judgment and also caused the nations to mourn over her (31:15).

EZEKIEL'S FUNERAL DIRGE OVER EGYPT (32:1-16)

A dirge is a musical composition expressive of grief, accompanying funeral rites. Egypt was going to die (31:16-18). In Yahweh's grief over the iniquity of Egypt, He asked Ezekiel to lift up a dirge concerning Pharaoh (32:2).

The dirge in verses 1-15 is a fitting summary of the judgment messages which Ezekiel had announced upon Egypt. Nebuchadnezzar would devastate the pride (cf. chap. 31) of Egypt. Egypt as both a "young lion" on the land and a "monster in the seas" (ASV) would be snared with the net of the king of Babylon and hurled upon the dry land as carrion for the birds and animals (vv. 2-5; cf. 29:5; 31:13). She would be humbled (cf. 31:12) and her bloodshed would water the mountains and fill the stream beds (v. 6). God would darken the heavens when

Egypt was destroyed (vv. 7-8; cf. 30:3, 18), and nations would be provoked, appalled, and troubled when the news of Egypt's destruction was brought to their lands (vv. 9-10).

The daughters of the nations, like the professional mourners of that day, would sing a funeral dirge over Egypt's death too—perhaps Ezekiel's dirge. Yet, even in the dirge, Yahweh reminded the hearers that His purpose was to make Himself known through His judgment (v. 15).

The surety and finality of the fall of Egypt, symbolized by this funeral dirge, are declared by Ezekiel (in March, 585 B.C.) only six months after the fall of Jerusalem to Babylon. What a somber time this must have been!

EZEKIEL'S LAMENT OVER EGYPT AND HIS FINAL INVITATION TO ISRAEL (32:17—33:20)

Since Ezekiel had been following a basic chronological scheme, the date of this section, like that of the first part of chapter 32, may create questions. Why did Ezekiel vary from this chronological approach? Editorial reasons seem to be the answer. The basic chronological thrust of the book is still present, centering around the pivotal point of the fall of Jerusalem. The two oracles (32:1-16; 32:17—33:20) which conclude the announcement of judgment upon Egypt were received from Yahweh and delivered approximately six months after Jerusalem's fall. Why? First, God was reminding Egypt that though Jerusalem and Judah had fallen, God was not finished; He would still carry out His prophecies of judgment against Egypt. In verses 1-16, Yahweh's lament gave a concluding summary of Egypt's collapse. Then, in 32:17—33:20, Yahweh delivered a warning message through Ezekiel to the exiles in Babylon.[1] By the time they received this final exhortation from Ezekiel, they already would have heard the messages of hope which announced the future restoration of Israel to Palestine (33:21—39:29). The Jewish exiles had obviously done some thinking in the four months since they heard of Jerusalem's fall and Ezekiel delivered his messages of hope.

1. The last messages in Ezekiel are chronologically arranged as follows: (1) Eze 33:21—39:29 was delivered in Dec./Jan. 586/5, B.C.; (2) Eze 32:1-16 was spoken in Mar., 585 B.C.; (3) Eze 32:17—33:20 was proclaimed in Apr., 585 B.C., fifteen days after Eze 32:1-16; and (4) Eze 40-48 was given in Mar./Apr., 573 B.C.

They probably wondered about their present status. Jerusalem had fallen; restoration was future. But what would be their fate now as exiles in Babylon? The message in 33:1-20 answers that cry.

Why did Ezekiel editorially arrange his messages in the manner that he did? Why did he not place this message, and that in verses 1 through 16, in their proper chronological order, after chapter 39 and before chapter 40? These messages are not arranged chronologically because (1) Ezekiel wanted to complete the warnings of judgment before he announced the messages of hope (33:21—39:29), and (2) he wanted to keep the messages of judgment upon Egypt together as a unit (similar to the reason for placing 29:17—30:19 in its place). Ezekiel employed both a chronological and a topical development in his book.

Two separate messages are included in 32:17—33:20. The first concerns the final lament over Egypt (32:17-32). The power of God's word is demonstrated in a lament, for in verse 18 the Lord actually commanded Ezekiel to cause Egypt to go down to the pit, to Sheol. Egypt would suffer that same ultimate fate of all nations who rebel against Yahweh. Her pride would be crushed. She would be unlovely and would lie in the pit of Sheol with the uncircumcised whom she considered beneath her dignity.

Ezekiel listed the mighty nations who had gone down to Sheol before Egypt: Assyria (Asshur); Elam, who had joined Assyria against Jerusalem (Is 22:6; cf. Jer 49:34-38); Meshek and Tubal, around the Black and Caspian seas; Edom; and the Sidonians. The emphasis of the lament was to show that Egypt would go down to Sheol as surely as those nations had (v. 29). Egypt may have found relative comfort in the fact that she would not be alone, but this would be menial comfort in light of eternity.

Why had these nations and Egypt departed from this life and descended to Sheol? Each had caused terror in the land of the living, being cruel and violent to others on this earth, especially to Israel. However, Yahweh had now set His terror (judgment) in this earth in order to judge those who had caused terror (vv. 31-32).

The second message (33:1-20), delivered in April, 585 B.C. (cf. 32:17), echoes two previous sections of this book: (1) Ezekiel's commission as a watchman in chapter 3, and (2) the exhortation to individual responsibility in chapters 3 and 18. Ezekiel was commissioned to perform the role of a watchman for the nation of Judah, announcing the warnings of the coming judgment of Yahweh (Eze 3). He had faithfully performed that task in chapters 4 through 32. He sounded the trumpet of warning, but Judah did not heed that warning. Therefore she fell to the invasion of Babylon, God's instrument of judgment. He also had announced the coming of hope and restoration to the nation (33:21—39:29).[2]

Six months had passed since the fall of Jerusalem, and four months had elapsed since the exiles heard the messages of hope and blessing for future restoration to Canaan. Undoubtedly the exiles had given some thought to their status. God's purpose for judgment was being accomplished. This is certainly indicated in verse 10, where they finally recognized that the judgment had come because of their own sins as much as for the past sins of the nation. Previously, when Ezekiel delivered his message (chap. 18) on the individual's responsibility to decide for life or death by keeping or not keeping the Mosaic covenant, the people of Judah had declared that any judgment which Ezekiel pronounced upon them really was caused by their fathers' sins. They saw no individual wrong on their part. Now 33:10 indicates that their attitude had changed; they realized that the judgment also came because of their sins. Having heard the messages of future hope, they began to ask about their present situation. Would they live and how (33:10b)?

Ezekiel replied with the same gracious invitation as before. God's ways had not changed. The people of Judah had to turn from their wicked ways and walk according to Yahweh's statutes (33:11, 15-16). If they had done righteousness according to God's Law, they should not turn and do wickedness, for it would bring physical death.[3] In the Mosaic covenant God showed His people how to live. If they would not follow His ways, they would surely die. There is no time when an individual is to live apart from God's ways (vv. 12a, 13). Likewise, there is no time when a person cannot turn from his sin, walk in God's ways, and so experience the blessing of God's righteous ways (vv. 12b,

2. Cf. the chronology in note 1.
3. Cf. the discussion on "life" and "death" in chap. 18.

14-16, 19). Righteousness is not what one says he will do, but what he actually does. Ezekiel stressed that the people of Judah had to do the Law of God (vv. 14-15; cf. Ex 22:1-2; Num 5:7-8).

Though the similarity of 33:1-20 with 3:17-20 and chapter 18 is very strong, the emphasis in the former passages is as much on Ezekiel's responsibility to Judah as upon Judah's responsibility. In 33:1-20, the basic emphasis now lies on the individual's responsibility. Each person must make a decision. They cannot rely upon the past. At each moment they must decide to walk according to God's ways and so experience the blessing inherent in these ways. That invitation has always been open to Israel (cf. Deu 30:15-20). God will judge each one according to his own individual ways, not by his intentions and professions (v. 20).

4

THE FAITHFULNESS OF GOD AND JUDAH'S FUTURE BLESSINGS

33:21—48:35

NIGHT MESSAGES OF HOPE AND ENCOURAGEMENT
(33:21—39:29)

SUMMARY

Expositors normally make a major break in the argument of the book between chapters 32 and 33. This would be an artificial separation since there is no chronological notice at the beginning of chapter 33 and since 33:1-20 belongs to the section of judgment oracles upon the nations. In addition, the chronological notice, which normally begins a new section in this prophecy, occurs in 33:21. Thus a new thrust in Ezekiel's argument begins in verse 21.

One of the major topics in chapters 33-39 is the land of Israel. Why has the nation of Israel lost the homeland which Yahweh promised to Abraham, their father? To understand Yahweh's answer to this question requires a brief review of God's covenant program. The Abrahamic covenant (Gen 12:1-3) is God's basic program for blessing the world. In this covenant Yahweh promises that He will choose one man, through that one man He will create a nation (Israel), and through that nation of Israel He will bless the entire world.

The Mosaic covenant (Ex 20—Num 9; Deu) was given as Israel's constitution. It governs the entire way of life of the people of Israel as a nation. If they will obey the stipulations of the covenant, they will receive the blessing of their great King, Yahweh (Deu 28), and will appropriate the blessings of the Abrahamic covenant (Deu 7:12; 8:1), that is, they will be in the land of blessing (Israel) and will be a blessing to the world. However, if the nation of Israel is disobedient to the Mosaic covenant, she will experience the judgment and discipline of that covenant (Deu 28; Lev 26) and will not—at any given point in time—participate in the blessings of the Abrahamic covenant, that is, she will neither be in the land of blessing nor be a blessing to the world.

In 2 Samuel 7:12-16 God revealed His covenant to David, promising that his descendants would rule upon the throne of David always: an eternal throne over an eternal kingdom. The Davidic covenant is the basis for Israel's hope in *the* Messiah (the anointed One, the King) of the line of David who would ultimately come to rule over them and the world eternally (i.e., the Millennium).

Finally, both Jeremiah 31 and Ezekiel 36 proclaim a new covenant which is to come. It will be better than the Mosaic covenant and therefore replace the Mosaic covenant and its role. When the new covenant is instituted by the singular death of the Messiah once and for all, then Israel (and all who believe) will appropriate the blessings of the Abrahamic covenant through the new covenant rather than through the Mosaic covenant. The Law (the Mosaic covenant) will be written upon their hearts, and the Holy Spirit will be poured out upon them.

It is extremely important that the reader have these covenants firmly in mind as he studies the following chapters in Ezekiel. The emphasis in this portion of Ezekiel must be seen in the framework of Deuteronomy 29:1—30:10. Read this portion of Deuteronomy now before continuing in Ezekiel. Note the blessings for obedience to the Mosaic covenant and the judgment for disobedience. This is the issue which has its outworking in Ezekiel 33:21—39:29.

The date was December, 586 B.C. Jerusalem had lain in ruins for three months. Finally the fugitive from Jerusalem had reached Babylon to bring the news of this tragedy.

The fall of Jerusalem is pivotal to the book of Ezekiel. The messages of Ezekiel leading up to the destruction of this holy city have emphasized its judgment. When Ezekiel concluded his message of judgment upon Israel in chapter 24, he predicted that when Jerusalem fell, a fugitive would come and report the fall, at which time Ezekiel's peculiar dumbness would leave him as a sign to the nation of Israel (24:26-27). Ezekiel 33:21-22 described the actual fulfillment of that prophecy. Thematically, Ezekiel, as a watchman, had just finished an exhortation to the exiles to turn, as individuals, to Yahweh and live (33:1-20). Jerusalem had fallen! Was all lost? "No!" was Ezekiel's message. The basis for this emphatic declaration of hope was found in the promises of God's covenants.

Ezekiel 33:21—39:29 contains the messages that Ezekiel delivered the night prior to the coming of the fugitive from Jerusalem to declare his message. Verse 22 carefully declares that Ezekiel's mouth was opened on that evening and he spoke until the fugitive came in the morning. The content of his messages that night are contained in Ezekiel 33:21—39:29. Though there are six distinct messages, they are all intertwined to develop the singular proclamation of hope and ultimate blessing.

JERUSALEM FALLEN; SEPARATION FROM THE LAND (33:21-33)

The remnant of Judah still residing in Palestine was asking: What has happened? Is not the land ours according to God's promise to Abraham? If one person, Abraham, received the land, why are the many descendants now separated from this promised land (v. 24)?

The reply of the Lord was clear (vv. 25-29): As long as you disobey the Mosaic covenant by doing such things as eating blood (cf. Lev 17:10-14; 19:26), looking to idols (Ex 20:4-5; Eze 18:6), shedding blood (Ex 20:13; Eze 18:10), defiling your neighbor's wife (Ex 20:14; Eze 18:6; 22:11) or making abomination, you will reap the judgment of the Mosaic covenant which comes upon you to cause you to repent and to prove that I am Yahweh (cf. Deu 29:25-29).

Then the Lord turned Ezekiel's attention to the response of the Babylonian exiles to these messages (vv. 30-33). They came and sat before Ezekiel and heard his words, but they did not do them. Mockingly they exhorted one another to come hear the word from Yahweh (v. 30). Ezekiel was "fun" to listen to, like an appealing tune. His messages and actions were intriguing, captivating the exiles by what they considered to be good showmanship. But they did not take his warnings seriously, since their interest was only in those things that brought material gain. However, when Ezekiel's messages came to pass—and the exiles were beginning to see this occur in the destruction of Jerusalem—then the exiles would know the stark realization that a genuine prophet had been in their midst (v. 33). Perhaps they finally would listen.

FALSE SHEPHERDS OF ISRAEL; THE TRUE SHEPHERD (34:1-31)

Yahweh's reply (33:25-29) to the question of the remnant in Israel simply explained why Judah lost the land: God took her out of the land in faithfulness to His just judgments (Deu 28-30).

Now Yahweh would develop this concept as it related to Judah's leadership in Ezekiel's second message (chap. 34): "Your false shepherds will be judged for their failure to properly shepherd you, Israel, My flock. Therefore, I Myself will be your Shepherd."

This judgment oracle was divided into two sections: the accusation in verses 1-8, and the verdict in verses 9-31.

The accusation announced judgment upon the leaders of Israel who were represented by the figure of "shepherds." The reason for their judgment was explicit: they had fed upon the flock instead of feeding the flock. They had exploited the people of Israel for their own gain rather than meeting the needs of the people as a shepherd who cared for his flock. They had not healed individual members of the flock who were ill, nor lovingly brought back those who were outcasts; on the contrary, they had ruled with violence (vv. 2-4, 7-8). What was the result of their faulty shepherding? The flock strayed from God's ways and became food for every beast (nation). This was the expected result when a flock had no shepherd (vv. 5-6, 8).

The verdict was twofold: (1) Yahweh would be against the false shepherds (leaders) of Israel in judgment (vv. 9-10*a*); and (2) Yahweh, the true Shepherd, would become the Shepherd of Israel (vv. 10*b*-31).

The emphasis in the verdict was upon the work of the true Shepherd. Great stress was placed upon the fact that *Yahweh Himself* would become their Shepherd (vv. 11, 15). As a faithful Shepherd, He will gather the scattered flock (Israel) from foreign lands and restore them to their own land of Israel (the sheepfold) where He will feed and care for them (vv. 12-15). In contrast to the false shepherds, He will meet the individual needs of each sheep (v. 16; cf. v. 4). The bad "fat" sheep, rams, and he goats, the leaders of Israel who had exploited the flock, would be fed with judgment, for they had grown fat by eating the best portion of the pasture and drinking the clear water while trampling upon the rest of the pasture and polluting the remainder of the water for the other sheep (vv. 16-19). They had pushed aside and scattered the helpless diseased sheep (vv. 20-21). These proud leaders of Israel were just other members of the flock before Yahweh, the Judge and the new Shepherd. They no longer would be shepherds; they would be replaced. They were pictured as fat sheep, rams, and he goats which had violently abused the nation of Israel, their flock.

Then the Lord identified the person and work of the true Shepherd in clear covenant terms (vv. 22-31). The Shepherd is the Messiah, "My Servant, David, . . . their prince" (v. 25). This is the greater Son of David, his Descendant, the Messiah. The identity is clear when verses 13-16 and 23-24 are compared. The "Yahweh" of verses 13-16 is the "David" of verses 23-24. This is the Messiah, promised in the Davidic covenant, who will restore the nation of Israel to their land and shepherd them as His own flock. When this restoration has been completed, the covenant formula of the Mosaic covenant will be realized (v. 24): He will be their God, and they shall be His people. This will occur when Israel accepts the new covenant (Jer 31:33; cf. Ex 6:7; Deu 29:12-15).

At this point in Ezekiel's message, he revealed a new covenant which God would enter into with Israel in the day that He restored them to their land: the covenant of peace. Verses 25-31 describe the provisions of this neglected covenant. First, Yahweh will remove all foreign invaders and possessors from the land of Israel, likening them to beasts that prey upon the flock of Israel (vv. 25, 27-29). Second, in that day Israel will dwell securely in her land (vv. 25b, 27b-28). Third, Yahweh will make Israel and her land a blessing (vv. 26a-27a). Fourth, Israel will recognize ("know") Yahweh's sovereignty when He shatters the yoke which is upon them as exiles among the nations and delivers them in restoration (v. 27b). Fifth, Israel never again will be hungry in the land of Israel (v. 29b). Sixth, never again will Israel bear the shame of the nations (v. 29c). And finally, the covenant formula of the Mosaic covenant will be true: Yahweh will be their God; they will be His flock (vv. 30-31).

This peace covenant forms the skeletal outline of the following night messages of Ezekiel. Chapters 35-39 delineate the implementation of the covenant of peace in detail. Former possessors and future foreign invaders of the land were removed in 35:1—36:15 and 38:1—39:29, respectively. The security of Israel after her restoration to the land by the Messiah is further described in chapters 38-39. The restoration, with its accompanying blessings, recognition of Yahweh's sovereignty, and reunion of the nation of Israel with their true God, is fully detailed in 36:16—37:28. It is this covenant of peace, an eternal covenant, that will be established in the restoration (37:26). This covenant is viewed as already instituted, in part, in 38:11-13. The concluding summary of this entire message is given in 39:25-29, which summarizes the peace covenant.

A vital concern of this covenant of peace is the restoration of the land of Israel to the people of Israel. The remnant in Palestine had asked why the land was lost (33:24). Yahweh explained that it was lost temporarily and that the people were exiled from the land because of the disobedience of Israel and her leaders (33:22—34:31). Yet the Abrahamic and Mosaic covenants promise the land to Israel as a land of blessing. Therefore, the peace covenant explains how the land will be restored to Israel (36:16—37:28) and how those who have desired to possess the land will be removed (35:1—36:15). No one will ever again take the land of Canaan away from Israel once the peace covenant is instituted, not even Gog (chaps. 38-39).

Chapters 35 through 39 set forth the implementation of the covenant of peace.

JUDGMENT OF POSSESSORS OF THE LAND; ISRAEL AGAIN THE POSSESSOR (35:1—36:15)

The first development of the peace covenant in Ezekiel's six night messages concerned the removal of foreign possessors of the land (cf. 34:25-29). God was clearing the land of Israel of its continual invaders and possessors in preparation for the restoration of the people of Israel.

Emphasis was placed particularly upon the nation of Edom, perhaps as a poignant representative of all nations who had sought to occupy Israel. The age-long conflict between Esau (Edom) and Jacob (Israel) (cf. Mal 1:2-5) was set forth as the most significant example of this principle. Though this passage tends to look upon the "continual" animosity of Edom for Israel throughout the ages, stress also lies upon the future dominance of the land of Israel by Edom and Edom's consequential judgment. This germinal concept had already been put forth by Ezekiel in 25:14 (cf. Num 24:15-19; Is 11:11-16; Dan 11:41).

Following an introductory statement that Yahweh was against Edom in judgment (vv. 1-4), Ezekiel delivered a judgment speech against Edom in a series of two accusations (vv. 5, 10) and two verdicts (vv. 6-9, 11-15). Then, in 36:1-15, he followed a similar pattern in proclaiming yet a third judgment speech. This latter part of the message in 35:1—36:15 sets forth a prophecy of encouragement to the *land* of Israel.

The accusations and verdicts in 35:5-15 are summarized here now rather than treated separately. The reasons for judgment upon Edom were fivefold:

1. Edom had manifested continual enmity against Israel throughout her history (v. 5*a*; cf. Eze 25:12*b*).
2. Edom delivered Israel over to the execution of the sword by other nations in the time of Israel's past national calamities (cf. Ob 10-14). Edom also would hand Israel over to the sword during Israel's future iniquity of the end times (v. 5*b*; cf. 21:30-31; 25:14).
3. Edom had declared that she desired to possess the two nations, Israel and Judah (cf. 37:15-22). After Judah was taken captive to Babylon in 586 B.C., Edom moved into the Judean territory as far north as Hebron. It was John Hyrcanus, the Maccabean, who regained that area for the Jews (cf. 1 Mac 5:3, 65). It seems, from the passage under study, that Edom's desires for the land would continue until the end times.
4. Edom had blasphemed the mountains of Israel by saying, "they are laid desolate; they are given to us for food" (35:12, NASB; cf. Ob 16), yearning repeatedly to devour the people of Israel.
5. Edom had spoken against Yahweh (v. 13), and He had heard them.

The verdict of Yahweh was essentially that He would do to Edom as she had done to Israel (cf. Ob 15). It was retribution in kind. As the emphasis in the accusations was upon the incessant enmity of Edom against Israel, so the stress of Yahweh's judgment upon Edom (Mount Seir) would be to cause her to be a *continual* desolation and waste, never to be inhabited again 35:3, 4, 7-9, 14; cf. Ob 18; Eze 25:12-14; Jer 49:13, 18). When the whole earth is happy in the blessings of the Messianic Kingdom, Edom will be a desolation (v. 14). As Edom was happy when Israel was desolate, so Yahweh will be glad when Edom is desolate (v. 15). As Edom responded to Israel with hatred, anger, and jealousy, so Yahweh will respond to Edom in like manner (v. 11; cf. Ob 15). Though Edom hated bloodshed, it would pursue her, filling her land with the slain (v. 6; cf. Is 34:6-8; 63:1-6).

One resounding result of this verdict of judgment rings throughout the chapter. When all this occurred, then Edom would know that the Lord is Yahweh; they would recognize Him as Sovereign (35:4, 9, 15).

The second segment of this message concerns a judgment speech which in reality was a statement of encouragement to the *land* of Israel (36:1-15). This message is divided also in a series of two accusations (vv. 2-3, 13) and two verdicts (vv. 4-12, 14-15). The emphasis upon the verdict is obvious.

The accusation was fourfold: (1) The enemy (Edom and the residue of the nations in v. 5) claimed possession of the mountains of Israel, especially the ancient high places (vv. 2-3). (2) The residue of the nations had crushed Judah and caused her to be desolate (v. 3). (3) Oral defamation (an evil report) against Israel had been upon the lips of the foreign people (v. 4b). (4) The land was accused of devouring mankind and being bereft of her nation (v. 13). Again, the emphasis was upon possession, with its resulting cruelty and anti-Semitism.

The verdict was two-pronged, being introduced with the term "therefore" as it answered each of the accusations. The verdict began with a strong statement against Edom and the nations with her who joyously, and with despite, had possessed Israel for spoil. Yahweh, with fiery jealousy for His people, Israel, had announced judgment against these nations (v. 5). However, the keynote of this verdict lay in the encouragement to the *land* of Israel: (1) The land had borne the "shame of the nations" in the past, but she would no longer be known by that phrase nor bear the reproach of nations (vv. 5, 14-15). On the contrary, the nations would bear *their own* shame, their cruelty against

111

Israel as described in the accusation (cf. vv. 2-3; Eze 35:11-15; Ob 15). (2) The land would once again be productive, because Yahweh would make it fruitful as He prepared it for the return of His people (vv. 8-9). (3) *All* the house of Israel (not just a portion) would multiply on the land so that it would have more inhabitants than ever before (vv. 10-11). The land would be Israel's inheritance as promised under the Abrahamic covenant (v. 12*a*; Gen 12:7). (4) The land of Israel would never again be bereft of her people, Israel (v. 12*b*).

The emphasis of this entire message had been on the possession of the land of Israel. Yahweh was declaring that those who had sought, and were seeking, to possess the land of Israel would be removed and judged. In turn, Israel would possess her land once again as her inheritance, never again to be removed from it. The result of this verdict is interestingly stated in 36:11. The *land* of Israel will know the sovereignty of Yahweh when He fulfills His covenant promises to Abraham and Moses by restoring His people, Israel, to her land in the end times.

RESTORATION OF THE PEOPLE OF ISRAEL TO THEIR LAND
(36:16—37:14)

The emphasis in 36:1-15 was upon the land of Israel prospering again in preparation for the return of her people, Israel. That section provided a transitional bridge from the removal of foreign possessors of the land to the restoration of Israel to her rightful occupancy of Canaan. The salient feature of 36:16—37:14 is the restoration of the *people* of Israel as part of the peace covenant with Israel (cf. 34:26-29).

In order to grasp fully the magnificent goodness and grace of Yahweh in bringing Israel back to her land in the end times, Ezekiel initiated this message—typically begun with "And the word of Yahweh came unto me"—with a rehearsal of the past history of Israel which brought about her dispersion among the nations (36:16-21). In this setting, the gracious final restoration of Israel is described in verses 22-32, with the results of the restoration set forth in verses 33-38. Ezekiel concluded this message of restoration with an apocalyptic vision which he received as an encouragement to the exiles of his day. Yahweh would restore His people in the end times (37:1-14).

Ezekiel treated three factors in the discussion of Israel's past history which caused the dispersion. First, the reason for scattering the nation lay in her disobedience to God's will as revealed in the Mosaic covenant and the resulting defilement. These deeds specifically involved violent bloodshed and idolatry which rendered Israel as impure before God as an impure woman (36:17-18). After Yahweh dispersed His people in judgment, their very presence outside the land of Israel was then a pollution to the name of Yahweh. In the ancient Near East, each nation was closely associated with its own land. If they were driven from that land by other nations, the general understanding was that their god was insufficiently able to protect them. Therefore, Israel's presence in Babylon created the common opinion among the nations that Yahweh was not a strong God. It is in this sense that Israel profaned the name of Yahweh through her captivity (v. 20).

Second, Ezekiel clearly delineated that it was Yahweh who brought about the dispersion of Israel, judging them according to their deeds which violated the Mosaic covenant (vv. 18-19). In faithfulness to His covenant, Yahweh scattered the nation (cf. Deu 29:1—30:10) and allowed His name to be profaned.

The third element of Israel's past brings the reader to the final restoration which is outlined in the subsequent verses. The basis for the future restoration, as foretold in Deuteronomy 29:1—30:10, is Yahweh's compassion for His holy name which has been polluted by Israel among the nations (v. 21; cf. vv. 22-23, 32). This then provides a transition to the description of the restoration which immediately follows.

The second part of this message in 36:16—37:14 is the description of the final restoration (compare Ezekiel's previous discussion in 11:14-21). Ezekiel began by reemphasizing the basis of restoration. Yahweh will *not* bring Israel back to the land because of anything she has done, for when she returns she will loathe her past sins and be ashamed of them (vv. 31-32*b*). Israel will be returned to her land because of Yahweh's holy name which He Himself will sanctify among the nations; He will no longer allow His name to be polluted among all peoples (36:22-23; cf. vv. 21, 32). This was the same basis for the preliminary return of Israel from the Babylonian captivity, as set forth in Daniel 9:16-19. The wonderful outcome of this work of restoration will be that all the nations, including Israel, will recognize Yahweh's sovereignty (know Him) (36:23; cf. vv. 36, 38).

Ezekiel then outlined several marvelous facets of Yahweh's work of restoration:

1. Israel will be taken from *all* nations and lands where she has been dispersed and will be returned to the land of Israel (v. 24; cf. v. 19).

2. Once Israel has returned to her land, Yahweh will cleanse her from her idolatry (v. 25, 29a; cf. v. 33; 37:23; Jer 33:6-26). Since Ezekiel was a priest, the cleansing aspect will probably be a ceremonial cleansing, somewhat along the line of the cleansing for leprosy as outlined in Leviticus 14:5-7. Verses 26 and 27 of chapter 36 show how the Lord will cleanse His people. He will remove their old heart of stone, which went after other gods, and give them a new heart of flesh. In addition, He also will put a new spirit within them, the Holy Spirit of God, who will be poured out upon Israel in that day of restoration (cf. Eze 11:19-20; 18:31; 37:14; 39:29; Joel 2:28-29; 2 Co 3:3). This will occur when Israel accepts the new covenant (cf. Jer. 31:31-34). With the enablement of a new heart and Spirit, Israel will desire to walk in the ways of God which are enumerated in the Mosaic covenant (v. 27; cf. Jer 31:33; Ro 8:4; 2 Co 3).

3. The land promises of the Abrahamic covenant finally will be fulfilled. Israel will dwell in the land promised to her forefathers (v. 28a; cf. Gen 12:7).

4. The covenant formula of the Mosaic covenant ("I shall be your God, and you shall be My people") will be realized (v. 28b). Though the new covenant has replaced the Mosaic covenant by this time, the new covenant has not obliterated the Mosaic covenant. The Law will be written upon their hearts (Jer 31:33), and they will walk in the stipulations of the Mosaic covenant (cf. v. 27). Finally Israel will live before God in that proper relationship designed in her constitution, the Mosaic covenant.

5. Yahweh will make abundant provisions for His people through the phenomenal production of the land (vv. 29-30; cf. v. 35; Eze 34:29; Is 35:1-2). Never again will Israel experience famine.

Ezekiel concludes this section of his message by summarizing the effects of Israel's restoration both upon the nations and upon Israel. The surrounding nations will realize that the work of restoration is the work of Yahweh alone when they see the land of Israel, which had lain desolate for so long, become like the Garden of Eden (vv. 33-36). Israel will be increased as a holy flock for the divine Shepherd (cf. chap. 34). The restoration will cause the inhabitants of Israel to recognize Yahweh's sovereignty over them as their great king (vv. 37-38).

The apocalyptic vision in 37:1-14 is not a separate message. Ezekiel's normal method for introducing a new message (by the phrase "And the word of Yahweh came unto me") is not presented here. Rather this vision is a visual illustration of how the restoration will be accomplished. Apocalyptic literature is symbolic visionary prophetic literature, composed during oppressive conditions, consisting of visions whose events are recorded exactly as they were seen by the author and explained through a divine interpreter, and whose theological content is primarily eschatological.[1] These verses contain all of these necessary elements: (1) they employ symbols such as the dry bones; (2) this is the actual recounting of a vision seen by Ezekiel; (3) the passage, as part of the book of Ezekiel, is definitely prophetic; (4) Ezekiel composed this message during oppressive exilic conditions ; (5) the vision contains a divine interpretation; and (6) the content is eschatological.

Apocalytic literature has a very simple two-part form: (1) the setting of the vision; and (2) the vision per se with its divine interpretation. The vision is discussed with respect to these two elements.

The setting (vv. 1-2) was in the midst of the valley (or plain). This plain is not defined specifically anywhere in the passage. The only possible explanation might be that the article *the,* specifying a particular valley, may refer to the same valley in which Ezekiel saw his visions of God (cf. chap. 1). Ezekiel was the recipient of the vision; he was led through the valley—a valley full of many extremely dry bones—by the Spirit of Yahweh.

The vision which Ezekiel saw had two distinct sections: the vision per se in verses 3-10, and the interpretation in verses 11-14. These

1. Cf. Ralph H. Alexander, "Hermeneutics of Old Testament Apocalyptic Literature," p. 45.

two aspects of the vision are discussed simultaneously to enable the reader to understand the vision correctly.

Yahweh asked Ezekiel if the dry bones could live. Ezekiel, in turn, replied that only the Lord knew (v. 3). Then Yahweh commanded Ezekiel to prophesy to the bones, declaring that the Lord would reunite them into skeletons, place flesh and skin upon them, and breathe into them in order that they would live (vv. 4-6). Ezekiel obeyed the Lord, and the bones reunited to form the prophesied human beings. But there was no spirit (breath) in them (vv. 7-8). Then Ezekiel was required to prophesy to the breath to breathe upon the slain ones so that they would live (v. 9). This Ezekiel did, and the skeletons came alive when the breath came upon them, resulting in a great army (v. 10).

Unfortunately many commentators have sought to identify every detail of apocalyptic visions. This is not in keeping with the interpretation of the divine interpreters throughout biblical apocalyptic literature. Rather, a central message is to be discovered, and the divine interpretation must be closely followed without adding extraneous opinions.

The interpretation segment of this vision is relatively simple. The bones were the only symbol definitely identified, specifically in verse 11 and indirectly in verse 9. They represented the "whole house of Israel," the slain ones. Verse 11 relates that the bones declared that they were dry (a normal condition of the bones of those who have been dead for a long time) and their (Israel's) hope was perished. The bones (or members of the house of Israel) were separated from one another. The vision of the reunion of the separated bones into a great living army was simply the visual portrayal of the restoration of Israel which was discussed in 36:16-38. The divine interpreter declared this to be the case in verses 12-14 where he employed a new figure, that of resurrection from graves, to explain the regathering of the dry bones. The lesson is the same in both figures. Yahweh shall cause Israel to live again as a nation, physically (represented by the skeleton) and spiritually (represented by the breath, or Spirit—the same word in the Hebrew). Yahweh will bring Israel to her land (v. 12). He will restore her spiritually by placing His Spirit within her (v. 14; cf. 36:26-27) with the result that Israel will recognize Yahweh as her sovereign Lord (vv. 13-14).

Apocalyptic visions are for encouragement. The discouraged exiles could know that there was hope (cf. v. 11). First, Yahweh will restore His people to the land physically and then cleanse them spiritually. Note the order of the vision in verses 4 through 10 and the same order in the interpretation section (vv. 11-14). This is identical to the order found in 36:22-27 which described the rebirth of the nation of Israel. Now the rebirth of the nation is being illustrated by this apocalyptic vision. Once more the necessary elements for the existence of a nation are provided by Yahweh: a people has come into being as a unity (chaps. 36-37), a homeland is once again provided (36:1-15), and a government will be given (chaps. 40-48).

THE REUNION OF ISRAEL AND THE FULFILLMENT OF HER COVENANTS (37:15-28)

This message began like the others of Ezekiel, with the introductory phrase: "the word of [Yahweh] came again unto me." Ezekiel would perform a symbolic act, and then declare its meaning to his hearers. In interpreting the act, Ezekiel would summarize the restoration of Israel, demonstrating how all of her covenants will be fulfilled during this final regathering.

The symbolic act (vv. 16-17) was that of taking two sticks, writing the name of one of the formerly divided kingdoms of Israel on each: Joseph, Ephraim, and the house of Israel on one, representing the Northern Kingdom, and Judah on the other, representing the Southern Kingdom. The two sticks then became one in the hand of Ezekiel.

When asked the meaning of this symbolic act, Ezekiel was to respond as Yahweh had instructed him: This was the reuniting of the former kingdom of Israel and Judah into one nation (vv. 19-20, 22) restored to her promised homeland (vv. 21, 25) and cleansed from her idolatrous ways (v. 23a), with one King and Shepherd over the unified nation forever: "My servant David," the Messiah (vv. 22, 24a, 25b). The nation will be His vassal, walking in the requirements of the Mosaic covenant (v. 24b), and He shall be their great King according to the Mosaic covenant formula: "I will be your God, and you shall be My people" (cf. v. 23b). The people of Israel will dwell forever upon the land of Canaan (v. 25a; cf. Gen 17:8).

When all of Israel's covenants are fulfilled—the eternal land promises of the Abrahamic covenant realized (v. 25), the covenant formula of the Mosaic covenant operative as Israel walks in the stipulations of that covenant (vv. 23-24), cleansed under the new covenant (v. 23), and experiencing the eternal reign of her King, the greater Son of David, according to the Davidic covenant—then the peace covenant (v. 26; cf. 34:25-29) will have been fulfilled. All covenants to Israel will be accomplished at the time of her final restoration. At that time Yahweh will return to dwell in His sanctuary (cf. chaps. 40-48) in Israel as their God forever (cf. the departure of His glory from Israel in chap. 11 and its return in chap. 43). The final testimony (v. 28) is that all nations shall recognize Yahweh's sovereignty when He sanctifies Israel (sets her apart among the nations) by His presence in Israel forever.

THE FINAL ATTEMPT OF FOREIGNERS TO POSSESS THE LAND OF ISRAEL (38:1—39:29)

This was the final message in this series of six night oracles delivered by Ezekiel during the night preceding the arrival of the fugitive from Palestine with the news that the city of Jerusalem had fallen (33:21-22). A central concern throughout all these night messages had been the possession of the land of Israel. Foreign possessors had taken Jerusalem, the news of which would be reaching Ezekiel and the exiles by morning. This series of night oracles was given to encourage the exiles that ultimately God would remove these invaders and restore this land to Israel. Then He will enter into a covenant of peace with Israel, as described in 34:25-29 and 37:21-28.

Ezekiel 38 and 39 view the *entire* nation of Israel (after the restoration) dwelling securely in Messianic security, at peace (cf. 38:8, 11, 14; 39:26). The phrase "dwell safely" is clearly delineated in the book of Ezekiel as a description of Messianic security after Israel's restoration. This is specifically observed in the context of these night messages (cf. 34:25-29; 28:26) as well as in other prophetic contexts concerned with the Messianic end times (cf. Zec 14:11; Jer 23:6; 32:37; 33:16). Israel has entered into the peace covenant described in 34:25-29, living without walls, bars, or doors (38:7).

The time of the events in these two chapters is circumscribed by several chronological phrases and the general context. The end times are certainly in view. The phrase "after many days" (38:8) normally has the indefinite meaning "for a long time," though it is employed at times to reach as far as the end times (cf. Jer 32:14; Ho 3:4; Dan 8:26), as is true in this context. The phrase "in the [last] days" (38:16) places these events at the end times, since this phrase is normally used to refer to the time of Israel's final restoration and the rule of the Messiah (cf. Is 2:2; Jer 23:20; 30:24; Ho 3:5; Mic 4:1; Dan 10:14). "In the latter years" (38:8) is mentioned only this once in the Old Testament, but since this phrase is in the same verse as "after many days," one should interpret its meaning in light of that verse with its specific context of restoration. Ezekiel also declared that the events of these two chapters are to take place when the land of Israel is restored from the sword (38:8; cf. 36:1-15), and when the people of Israel have been gathered from many nations to the mountains of Israel (38:8, 12; cf. 36:22—37:14). All this, together with the whole emphasis in the series of night messages upon the final restoration of the people of Israel to their land, argues very strongly for these events to occur at the end times in conjunction with the restoration of Israel and her entrance into the peace covenant. A more specific discussion as to the exact place where these chapters fit into God's prophetic scheme of the end times is treated later.

The description in these chapters depicts a final attempt to possess the land of Israel, but without success, for Yahweh will defend Israel according to His eternal covenant of peace described fully in 34:25—37:28. Gog's defeat is a vindication of Yahweh's faithfulness to His covenant promises (34:29; cf. 37:22-28). Yahweh will not permit His holy name to be polluted any more by the dispersion of Israel (39:7; cf. 36:20).

The content of these two chapters is relatively simple to understand. However, as one studies these chapters he must keep in mind that 39:1-24 is essentially a statement and expansion of 38:1-23. Such a practice is common in judgment-speech literature toward the end of the history of Judah (i.e., sixth and fifth centuries B.C.).

Ezekiel 38:1-13 and 39:1-2 depict Yahweh bringing Gog and his great entourage from every part of the world (Persia from the east, Cush from the south, Put from the west, Gomer and Togarmah from the north, and the islands of the sea in the west) to the land of Israel. They all will enter the land together from the north after Israel is restored to her land and is dwelling in Messianic security (38:1-8; 39:6). The armies will come to spoil and plunder the land (38:9-13).

Ezekiel 38:14-17 is a brief portion not explicitly referred to in chapter 39. It declares that Yahweh will *bring* Gog upon the land in order that the nations may recognize His sovereignty ("know that I am Yahweh") when He is sanctified before them by destroying Gog. Yahweh asserts that this final invasion of Gog was mentioned through His prophets in former days. However, no explicit previous passage can be referred to as this former statement. Several prophets do make general mention of such an invasion at the end times (cf. Deu 30:7; Is 26:20-21; Jer 30:18-24).

Ezekiel 38:18-23 and 39:3-16 focus upon God's judgment against Gog and his hordes. The section may be divided into three aspects. In 38:18-22 (39:3) Yahweh's wrath against Gog is described. It will be accompanied by a shaking of the earth (38:19-20), a sword called for against Gog (38:21*a*), pestilence, bloodshed, fire, brimstone, and hailstones (38:22; 39:6). Yahweh will totally disarm the armies of Gog (39:3). Ezekiel 38:23 and 39:7, 21-24 set forth the results of this judgment: (1) The nations will recognize Yahweh's sovereignty and glory as He is magnified through His judgment against Gog and sanctified as the *Holy* One in Israel. (2) Israel will continue to recognize Yahweh's holy name in this event, for Yahweh *will not* permit His holy name to be polluted through the defeat and removal of Israel from her land by Gog. Then Israel will cleanse the land after Gog's defeat by burning the weapons of Gog's armies for seven years as fuel (39:8-10), spoiling those who spoil her (v. 10*b*), and burying the dead of Gog's hordes for seven months (vv. 11-16) in a valley east of the sea.

Scholars differ as to the location of the valley east of the sea in 39:11, the valley of trespassers ("passengers," or "passers-by," NASB). Many seek to change the word "trespassers" to "Aravah," thereby identifying the valley with the Jordan rift (the Aravah) and the sea as the Dead Sea. This, however, would put the valley outside of the boundaries of Israel as they are normally understood. Others see the valley as any valley east of the Mediterranean Sea in a more general sense. Though the author prefers the latter, neither position greatly affects the interpretation of the passage.

Ezekiel 39:17-20 pictures a "supper" to which the birds of the air and the beasts of the field are called. They eat the flesh and drink the blood of the carnage of Gog's defeated armies, especially the leaders who came with him (v. 18; cf. the use of animals to describe people in Is 34:6; Rev 19:17-19; cf. similar imagery in Jer 46:10).

Ezekiel 39:25-29 concludes this division of the book which has been concerned primarily with Israel's peace covenant and the entire series of six night messages (33:21—39:29). These final verses are a summary of the whole: (1) Israel will be restored after she bears the judgment for her iniquity and rebellion, at which time she will dwell securely with no one to cause her to tremble (vv. 25-27). (2) At that time Israel will recognize Yahweh's sovereignty in her midst (v. 28). (3) Yahweh will pour out His Spirit upon Israel (v. 29; cf. 36:27; 37:1-14; chaps. 40-48), never again to hide His face from Israel, as demonstrated in His supernatural protection of her in chapters 38 and 39.

The identification of Gog and the specific time of the events of these chapters are problems that have perplexed scholars for centuries. It is hoped that the arguments presented below will bring us closer to a more accurate solution.

The identity of Gog and the more explicit time relation of these chapters are intertwined. The etymological data for the term "Gog" is extremely uncertain. Lacking such, several solutions have been proposed: (1) *Gugu,* one Gyges, king of Lydia who reigned a century before Ezekiel; (2) *Gagu,* a ruler of the land of Sakhi, an area north of Assyria; (3) *Gaga,* a mountainous land north of Melitene; (4) A term which is derived from the other associate word "Magog"; and (5) an official title, based on the Septuagint rendering of several kingly names in the Old Testament (cf. Num 24:7; Deu 3:1, 13; 4:47; Amos 7:1), and perhaps employed as a general name for any enemy of God's people at the time of the composition of the Septuagint. None of the above solutions possess any significant support to warrant acceptance as the answer for Gog's identity. The most that can be said, perhaps, is that Gog is probably a personage, whether described by title or by name. Further speculations are not warranted on the basis of the Old Testament data presently available. Of necessity a final discussion of this issue must be delayed until after the treatment of the time element.

121

Other names in these chapters also attract the interest of the student who would seek to know their identification. "Magog," associated with the Japhetic line in the table of nations in Genesis 10, is referred to by Josephus (*Antiquities of the Jews*, 1. 6. 1) as the Scythians who lived in an area around the Black and Caspian seas. This view is most generally accepted. The phrase "chief prince of Meshech and Tubal" has elicited a variety of comments and identities. The term "chief" (or "Rosh") causes more trouble than any other word in this phrase. The Hebrew word is *rosh*. The normal meaning is "head" or "chief." Some, however, prefer to render the Hebrew term as a proper name of a geographical location called Rosh. Those arguing to the contrary would observe that no such country is ever mentioned elsewhere in the Old Testament or in extrabiblical material. In addition, Meshech and Tubal, normally mentioned together in Scripture and generally accepted to be countries located in the general area of contemporary Turkey, are not associated with the term *rosh* either within or outside of Scripture, whether or not *rosh* is conceived as a proper name (cf. Gen 10:2; 1 Ch 1:5, 17; Eze 27:13; 32:26). Some understand *rosh* to mean modern Russia, but this identity has no basis. Those holding such a view normally appeal to etymology based on similar sounds (to the hearing) between the two terms, but such etymological procedure is not linguistically sound at all. The term Russia is a late eleventh-century A.D. term.

The accepted Hebrew text with its accents and construction strongly points to an appositional relationship between the terms "prince" and "chief" (*rosh*). Both (chief and prince) would relate then to the terms "Meshech" and "Tubal" in the same manner. This type of construction is common in the Hebrew language (cf. Is 37:22; 23:12; Jer 14:17; 46:9; 1 Sa 28:7; etc., and *Gesenius' Hebrew Grammar*, p. 422). Grammatically it would seem best to render the phrase as "the prince, the chief (or ruler) of Meshech and Tubal."

With these preliminary identifications understood, the more perplexing problem of the time of these events in the prophetic program of the end times must be treated.[2] Enough has been said above to demonstrate that

2. For further discussion of this issue, compare Ralph H. Alexander's "A Fresh Look at Ezekiel 38 and 39," *Journal of the Evangelical Theological Society*, vol. 17, no. 3 (Summer 1974), pp. 157-69.

the general time of these matters is most certainly the end times of history, especially that time which relates to Israel's restoration to her land. Therefore, only major futuristic positions should be considered. Each interpretation is briefly summarized along with its chief support. Since there are many variations within each position, only the basic concepts of each is treated. Then objections to each interpretation are set forth and evaluated. A correct solution should (1) follow a normal grammatical-historical hermeneutic, (2) fit the details of Ezekiel 38 and 39, not glossing over anything, (3) allow the primary time element to come from the Ezekiel passage, and (4) keep hypotheses to a minimum.

The first view declares that the events of Gog and Magog will occur before the Tribulation. The major argument put forth in favor of this position is that the concept of "dwell securely" is only explicable if the insecurity of the Tribulation has not yet begun. With essentially little in favor of this position, critics quickly object as follows:

1. The phrase "dwell securely" is often employed, especially in Jeremiah and Ezekiel, to refer to millennial security.
2. The context of these two chapters is the complete restoration of Israel to her own land, an event which will not transpire until Israel is freed "from the sword" at the end of the Tribulation.
3. The imminency of the rapture is ruled out if the event of Gog must precede the Tribulation, unless there is an adequate transition period.
4. Ezekiel 39:7, 22 declares that Yahweh's name will not be polluted again, a fact that is hardly possible in light of the forthcoming Tribulation.
5. The concept that the nations and Israel "know Yahweh" in the sense of recognizing His sovereignty would fit best in the context of the final universal knowledge of the Messiah by all nations when the Messiah has returned (38:16, 22; 39:7, 21, 23-24), rather than prior to the Tribulation.

Each of these objections is argued strongly on a biblical basis. Therefore, the author rejects this position.

A second major answer to the time problem is that the events transpire in the middle of the Tribulation. In support of this position the proponents state that Gog's invasion is to be equated with the invasion by the king of the north (Dan 11:40-41), which precipitates the Antichrist's severance of his covenant with Israel in the middle of the Tribulation period. The invasion occurs when Israel is dwelling in her own land, enjoying a false security of relative peace provided by her covenant with the Antichrist. The proponents of this position state that the invasion and destruction of Gog become a sign to the nations and Israel, causing them to "know" Yahweh in the midst of the Tribulation, a fact which supposedly agrees with the book of Revelation, which declares that *many* are saved at that time. Likewise, since Gog is the king of the north, and since he is not mentioned in Revelation 19:20 along with the demise of the beast and the false prophet, he must have been destroyed previously, that is, in the middle of the Tribulation.

In reply, expositors raise the following objections:

1. There is no biblical basis for the identification of Gog with the king of the north.
2. The concept of "false security" is both inconsistent with the purpose of the Tribulation (a time of Israel's chastisement and punishment) and contrary to the normal usage of the phrase "dwell securely" in Ezekiel. In addition, 39:26 (cf. 34:28 and Mic 4:4, employing the phrase in a millennial context) asserts that during the time of dwelling securely, there is no one causing terror, which is incongruous with the whole thrust of the Tribulation.
3. The burning of weapons and burying of bodies to cleanse the land, while the abomination of desolation (39:9-16) is occurring and judgment is at its peak, is inconceivable. Cleansing, in the immediate context of Ezekiel, is related to the national conversion of Israel (cf. chaps. 35-37).
4. Ezekiel 38:8, 16 seems to argue that the restoration from the sword has brought Israel into Kingdom blessing. That is certainly out of character with the Tribulation.
5. The declarations of 39:7, 22, 26 that Yahweh's name will never be polluted again and that there will be no one causing terror are antithetical with the Tribulation period.
6. The emphasis on Israel's prosperity in 38:11-12 is out of place in the time of her punishment during Daniel's seventieth week.
7. It is God, not the Antichrist, who destroys Gog.

Therefore, the author would acknowledge the overwhelming argument against this position as both biblical and also in keeping with normal hermeneutics and the details of the passage under consideration.

The third interpretation places the time of these events at the end of the Tribulation. Gog's armies are looked upon as included among those that gather together against Christ in Zechariah 12 and 14:1-4. Some holding this position identify Gog with the personage in Daniel 11:40, while others disassociate Gog from the Battle of Armageddon, postulating that these chapters describe a final battle at the end of the Tribulation *prior* to the judgment of Matthew 25 and the Millennium. These adherents maintain that the "dwelling safely" is a false security, based on Israel's wealth (cf. Eze 38:11-12).

Many of the objections to the mid-Tribulation position are leveled also against this position. Rather than reiterate those objections at this point, the reader should review objections (2), (4), (5), and (6) listed against the mid-Tribulation position. The concept of a false security is even more difficult to accept during the time of Armageddon at the end of the Great Tribulation than in the middle of the Tribulation where it was deemed incongruous. This interpretation does not harmonize well with the millennial aspects which characterize the period prior to the invasion of Gog (Eze 38:8, 16) nor with the idea of the land being restored from the sword (38:8). The author finds the weight of these objections too heavy to accept this proposition for the solution of the time element. Too many of the details in Ezekiel 38 and 39 conflict with this position.

Some expositors maintain that this invasion of Gog transpires during a transition period which follows the second advent but precedes the establishment of the Millennium. The strongest argument in favor of this view is the formidable allusion in Revelation 19:17-18 to the "bird supper" in Ezekiel 39:17-20. It is certainly the habit of the apostle John to base his arguments and imagery upon salient events and figures in the Old Testament, especially in the Prophets. This mention of a "bird supper" in Revelation 19 is inexplicable apart from the reference in Ezekiel 39. Such a strong allusion must be considered by students of both passages.

Devotees also argue that the phrases "dwell securely" and "latter days" are perfectly in keeping with the Messianic peace and restoration of Israel in the land following the end of the Tribulation. No one is causing them terror at this time. Contextually, Ezekiel 38 and 39 record the climax of the events connected with Israel's restoration in 33:21—39:29. The covenants to Israel are fulfilled (cf. 36:24; 37:12, 14; 34:24; 37:24-25; 36:26-27; 37:26); she has been restored to her land in prosperity and wealth (38:11-12) which harmonizes with the Messiah's presence (cf. Is 61:6). This is the picture described in Ezekiel 38:1-13 and 39:1-2 when Gog invades the land. The transition period allows sufficient time for the burning of weapons and burial of bodies for the cleansing of the land.

Yahweh's judgment in Ezekiel 38-39 corresponds to the treading of the winepress of wrath in Revelation 19:15. The sword which the Lord calls for against Gog in Ezekiel and the sword coming forth out of the Lord's mouth in Revelation both strike the nations coming against Yahweh and the land (cf. Eze 38:21 and Rev 19:15, 20). Revelation 19:19-21 states that it is the "beast" and his armies who attack the Lord at His second coming. Therefore Revelation 19:17-21 would imply that the "beast" and his armies of the Revelation should be identified with Gog and his hordes in direct fulfillment of Ezekiel 38 and 39 (cf. 38:4-7, 9, 15, 22; 39:4, 11 with Rev 19:15, 18, 19, 21). The demise of the "beast" in Revelation is the fulfillment of the fall of Gog in Ezekiel 38 and 39. John only summarizes the details given in the Ezekiel passage.

Objections brought forth against this position are relatively few. Many would argue that the biblical data to describe a transition period between the Tribulation and the Millennium is practically nonexistent. Therefore, much of the support for this position is based on hypotheses which can neither be proved, nor necessarily disproved. This is admittedly a weakness. Also, some would raise the question of how Gog escapes from the Battle of Armageddon. What nations would be present to observe the destruction of Gog described in Ezekiel 38:16, 22-23; 39:5-7, 21-24? How could Israel be dwelling securely in the land so quickly?

Plausible solutions are available to answer the objections: (1) nowhere is it stated that "the beast" is at the Battle of Armageddon; (2) the Battle of Armageddon does not require all the nations of the earth to be present, so that other nations would remain to observe Gog's fall; and (3) nothing requires that all these events transpire immediately. A transition period is most probable (cf. Mt 25). The formidable allusion of Revelation 19:17-21 to Ezekiel 39:17-20 cannot be thrust aside. The comparative study of these two passages seems to give strong support for acceptance of this position. It is hard to argue against this interpretation.

A final solution is put forth for the problem of the time of the events in Ezekiel 38 and 39; these events occur after the Millennium. The strong basis for this position is the explicit reference to Gog and Magog in Revelation 20:8. Such an explicit reference cannot be dismissed lightly, as is often the case. The terms employed in Revelation 20:8 are the same as those in Ezekiel 38 and 39. Normal hermeneutics would require the identification of the two passages (since the terms Gog and Magog are used nowhere else in the Scriptures) unless strong reasons can be brought forth to deny such an equation. The phrase "dwell safely" is certainly satisfied by this position since Ezekiel's normal use of the phrase is millennial in nature and this event of Revelation 20 is at the end of the Millennium. Nations from among those in the Millennium would be present to observe the destruction of Gog in fulfillment of Ezekiel 38:16, 21-23; 39:7, 21. There would be sufficient time for the burning of weapons and burial of bodies to cleanse the land; nothing argues against the cleansing of the land at this time. Certainly prosperity would be Israel's part in the millennial Kingdom (cf. Is 11, 35).

Many expositors quickly cast aside this possible equation of Ezekiel 38 and 39 with Revelation 20:8 and then struggle to explain the use of Gog by John. The major objections against this solution are: (1) Gog, in Ezekiel, is a northern coalition; in Revelation the armies come from the four corners of the earth. (2) Ezekiel says nothing of Jerusalem, whereas John declares that the nations encompassed the beloved city. (3) Disposal of the bodies and weapons seems to militate against this equation, since the great white throne judgment immediately follows the Millennium. Other lesser arguments are also asserted.

These objections are not impressive. For instance, the relation of the "four corners of the earth" in Revelation to the "northern coalition" in

Ezekiel is answered in Ezekiel 38:5-6 by kingdoms from the east (Persia), south (Cush), west (Put and the islands of the sea), and the north (Togarmah and Gomer) gathered by Gog to invade Israel from the north. John's mention of the "beloved city" does not disagree with Ezekiel, who declares that Gog comes upon the mountains of Israel, which most certainly would include Jerusalem (39:4-5). The argument against the disposal of the bodies and the burning of weapons due to the great white throne judgment immediately following the Millennium carries little weight. There is no demand in Scripture for an immediate sequence of events. A transition period is equally plausible. Therefore, the author finds no sufficient argument against this position.

The reader is perhaps a bit puzzled at this point. Two positions have been recognized as being fulfillments of the Ezekiel 38 and 39 passage. This is exactly what the author proposes. The hermeneutical principle of double fulfillment declares that a given prophecy may have both a near and a far fulfillment, two near fulfillments, or two far fulfillments. It is the latter that is proposed. Ezekiel 38 and 39 have a double fulfillment in Revelation 19:17-21 and 20:8. Revelation 19 finds the fulfillment in the demise of the beast, the chief instrument of Satan (similar to Eze 28:1-10). Revelation 20 finds the fulfillment in Satan, *the Gog* (similar to Eze 28:11-19), the enemy of Israel who makes the final attempt to regain the land of Israel from God's chosen people. The double fulfillment is found in two similar events with the last and greatest enemies of the people of Gog. The former, in one sense, prefigures the latter.

The full description of the events is recorded in Ezekiel. In the book of Revelation, John only summarized the events in each case since his readers would have been familiar with Ezekiel 38 and 39. The allusion to the "bird supper" is employed in Revelation 19 in order not to confuse the identity of the beast's demise by changing terminology from his readers' familiarity with the term "beast" to "Gog." Otherwise they may not have identified the "beast" with the "Gog" invasion, but might have perceived them as two separate events, since the last previous reference to the "beast" was in Revelation 17. However, in Revelation 20, the explicit reference is made by saying that "the Gog" is Satan. Therefore, "Gog" refers both to the "beast" of Revelation (chap. 19) and to

Satan (chap. 20). These events occur between the end of the Tribulation and the beginning of the Millennium (Rev 19), and after the Millennium (Rev 20), respectively. This, then, is a double fulfillment! It is regrettable that neither the position with a strong allusion nor the position with an explicit reference have ever been given much attention by evangelical scholars.

THE RETURN OF THE GLORY OF GOD (40:1—48:35)

INTRODUCTION

This is one of the most perplexing and difficult prophetic passages in Scripture. In many ways, however, this prophecy is only as difficult as one chooses to make it. If one abandons a normal grammatical-historical-cultural hermeneutic in favor of a figurative approach when studying this passage, he most certainly will encounter extreme difficulty. Figurative interpretation (often called *spiritual,* though far from the latter) has as its final criterion the subjectivity of man's mind, resulting in as many interpretations as there are interpreters. Who can dispute the results of "spiritual" interpretation, for the student, himself, is always the authority? Confusion abounds!

On the contrary, if one is willing (1) to lay his preconceived ideas aside, (2) to believe that the biblical text is accurately revealed, though it discusses things beyond the normal experience and understanding of mankind, and (3) to approach the text in a normal grammatical-historical-cultural way, he will discover that this passage is not nearly as difficult as he may have thought.

However, some who do follow a normal interpretive process still may tend to have problems. Upon completion of the study from a normal literal approach, the student may *feel* that what the passage declares is not *spiritual* enough, that it seems too factual and needs something more for the heart. At that point the student may turn to *spiritualizing* in order to make the text more "meaningful." This should not be done.

Following the interpretive methodology of "spiritualization" has given rise to several commonly held views of Ezekiel 40-48.[3] Failure

3. For a more complete discussion of interpretations of Eze 40-48 see M. F. Unger, *Great Neglected Bible Prophecies,* pp. 57-63; C. L. Feinberg, *The Prophecy of Ezekiel: The Glory of the Lord,* pp. 233-39; and James M. Gray, *Christian Workers' Commentary on the Old and New Testaments,* pp. 265-66.

to observe the future context of the passage, the apocalyptic nature[4] of the literature, and the testimony of past history, has caused many to misunderstand these chapters. Some interpret this passage as Solomon's Temple, the Temple constructed by Zerubabbel upon his return from the Babylonian captivity (either real or proposed), or Herod's Temple at the time of Christ's first coming. Others, accepting almost none of the text as literal, take most elements of the passage as purely symbolic of the Christian Church and its earthly blessings and glories. Even among those holding to a normal literal hermeneutic, failure on their part to examine and compare the parallel prophetic passages carefully has led them to identify Ezekiel 40-48 with the eternal state described in Revelation 21-22.

A normal grammatical-historical-cultural method of interpretation does not eliminate all problems of interpretation, but the questions remaining are minimal: (1) the relation of Ezekiel 40-48 to Revelation 21-22, (2) the question of sacrifices in the Millennium, and (3) the apocalyptic nature of the text of Ezekiel 40-48.

The initial issue concerns the place of Ezekiel 40-48 in the prophetic program. Many competent expositors have concluded that these chapters describe the eternal state of Revelation 21-22, while other equally qualified students of the Scriptures argue that Ezekiel's vision belongs to the millennial Kingdom. The author agrees with the latter position (the Millennium), basing this conclusion upon an examination and comparison of the details of Ezekiel 40-48 with Revelation 21-22.

Though there are similarities between the two—such as the twelve gates of the city of Jerusalem with the names of the twelve tribes of Israel, the recipient of the vision being on a high mountain, the messenger in the vision possessing a measuring rod to measure structures, and the stream flowing to the east for the healing of the land—the disparity between the two texts is greater and demands their disassociation.

For example, both segments describe a river (47:1-12; Rev 22:1-2), yet the stream issues from the Temple in Ezekiel (which is not in Jerusalem, see fig. VII) and from the city of Jerusalem and the throne of God in Revelation. In Ezekiel the throne of God is in the Temple (43:7), while in Revelation it is in Jerusalem (Rev 22:3). Though

4. For future elaboration of apocalyptic literature, see the discussion of Eze 37: 1-14.

in both Revelation and Ezekiel there is no temple in the city (Eze 48:8-22; Rev 21:22), in Ezekiel the Temple and Jerusalem are two separate identities. In Revelation there is no temple structure at all.

The measurements of the two cities are not the same, regardless of how one seeks to understand the shape of the city of Jerusalem in Revelation (Eze 48:30-35; Rev 21:15-17). In the Ezekiel context, the tribes of Israel are apportioned land with the sea as the western boundary, whereas in Revelation the sea is declared to no longer exist (Eze 47:15-20; Rev 21:1b). These discrepancies are sufficient to divorce the meaning of the two passages.

Though Ezekiel 40-48 refers to the Millennium and Revelation 21-22 to the eternal state, one may tend to feel uneasy in separating the two passages because of their distinct similarities and the normal policy of the apostle John to allude often to Old Testament prophetic passages in the book of Revelation. These similarities occur because both the Millennium and the eternal state are part of Israel's time of future blessing. Old Testament prophets often saw the future time of blessing into which the nation of Israel would enter as including all of what the apostle John distinctly separates into the Millennium (Rev 20) and the eternal state (Rev 21-22). This is illustrated in Isaiah 65:17 and 66:22 (cf. 2 Pe 3:10-13) which speak both of the new heavens and the new earth as well as of traits of the Millennium. Ellison observed that "the Millennium is the antechamber of and the preparation for the eternal state. Its glories are less than those of eternity, but they are of the same nature."[5] In other words, God's time of blessing is eternal. It starts at the beginning of the Millennium and continues into the eternal state, interrupted briefly by the cataclysmic events of Gog's fall, the great white throne judgment, and the destruction of the present heaven and earth after the first one-thousand years. The Millennium has specific purposes in God's program, such as to demonstrate the presence of sin even in a state of perfect environment. Yet, the eternal state is the ultimate of God's blessing to those who believe—a time of no sin and no death. The similarity of the twelve gates with the names of the twelve tribes of Israel in the city of Jerusalem in Ezekiel 40-48 (Millennium) and in Revelation 21-22 (eternal state) simply notes the fact that Israel shall

5. Henry L. Ellison, *Ezekiel: The Man and His Message,* p. 142.

be present during both periods. Equally, the two streams have a relationship to Genesis 2:9-10 where a river supernaturally flowed out of the Garden of Eden to bring blessing to the earth during that time of perfect environment. Likewise, in the Millennium (Eze 40-48) and in the eternal state (Rev 21-22), the source of life and blessing to the earth (whether the renovated old earth of the Millennium or the new earth of the eternal state) is from the throne of God and flows by means of a supernatural river.

A major obstacle to many expositors in their interpretation of Ezekiel 40-48 is the detailed description of a sacrificial system like the Mosaic system. A reenactment of the Mosaic sacrificial procedure in the Millennium would seem to contradict the New Testament teaching of Christ's death as a finished and complete work (Heb 7:17; 9:12, 25-28).

Several factors must be observed in response to this objection to a normal literal interpretation of the texts involved. First, Old Testament sacrifices *never* were efficacious (cf. Heb 10:3-4), neither in the Old Testament nor in the New Testament. The individual in Old Testament times was saved by faith in the finished work of the Messiah (Christ), which was to be accomplished in the future, but was portrayed in the Old Testament sacrifices and feasts, just as one today is saved by faith in the finished work of Christ that has been fulfilled historically on the cross. The Old Testament believer looked forward in faith; the New Testament saint looks back in faith. The object of faith for *everyone* is Christ, the Messiah. The sacrificial system of the Mosaic covenant pictorialized the work of Christ in order that the Israelite might understand what the Messiah would accomplish on man's behalf. But a sin offering, or a Day of Atonement, never provided eternal effectual salvation for anyone.

Second, the millennial sacrificial system is mentioned not only in Ezekiel, but also in Isaiah (56:5-7; 60:7, 13; 66:20-23), Jeremiah (33:15-22), and Zechariah (14:16-21).

Third, there is no retrogression in God's program. The barrier between Jews and Gentiles, which was removed by Christ, according to Ephesians 2:14-16, will not be reerected because of the millennial worship procedures. A full-blown Mosaic system is not reinstated in the place of the new covenant in the Millennium. Instead, the millennial worship appears to be pictorial lessons to everyone in the Millennium, just as it should be to us today (Ro 15:4; 1 Co 10:1-12). They are to remind us (and those in the Millennium) of the work which Christ performed for us and the life which we are to live. They are commemorative in the same manner as the Lord's table (cf. 1 Co 11:23-26).

Fourth, the sacrificial system described in Ezekiel is similar, though not identical, to the Mosaic system. Not all Old Testament feasts and pieces of Temple furniture are included. One may say that this is an argument from silence, but the omission of such elements as the Ark of the Covenant, the feast of Pentecost, and the Day of Atonement are not insignificant in comparing the two systems. Details differ as to the number and kinds of animals sacrificed (e.g., no lamb is offered in the Passover in the Millennium; more bullocks and rams are offered in the millennial feast of unleavened bread than in the Mosaic system, etc.). The priestly ministry in the millennial worship is conducted by the sons of Zadok (cf. Eze 40:46; 43:19; 44:15). Finally, there is no high priest in the Millennium. Instead, the prince[6] acts as both ruler and priest, a representative of the people as was the high priest in the Mosaic pattern.

These and other distinctions between the Mosaic and millennial programs are sufficient to repudiate any wedding of the two worship systems. Thus, a new worship program is instituted for the Millennium. Though it is similar to the Mosaic system and is primarily enacted for the culmination of God's purposes with His people Israel, the millennial worship program is distinct and unique, a pictorial ritual for all participants in the Millennium.

Fifth, the total argument of the book of Ezekiel must not be forgotten as one approaches these last chapters. It is imperative to remember that Ezekiel began this book by displaying the glory of God which Israel had defied and polluted by her abominable practices of disobedience to His holy Law, the Mosaic covenant. Ezekiel, the priest, emphasized the importance of properly following the regulations of the Law in every area. Israel failed miserably in this respect. As a result, the glory of God departed from Israel, from her Temple and her holy city, Jerusalem (Eze 8:3; 10:19; 11:23). When Yahweh has cleansed Israel and re-

6. See discussion of the "prince" below in the discussion of Eze 45.

stored her to the land and to her promised blessings, Israel will worship Yahweh correctly in a commmerative way according to the new worship program. All the covenants are fulfilled in the Millennium (cf. Eze 37: 23-26). It should not be surprising, therefore, to see commemorative elements similar to the Mosaic system in millennial worship (cf. Jer 31:33).

The last major interpretive issue concerns the apocalyptic nature of these nine chapters. *Apocalyptic* is a term which has been tossed to and fro by scholars to mean a variety of different things, basically anything visionary, symbolic, and futuristic. Such a loose definition is certainly out of order, especially in light of research which demonstrates that the term properly refers to a type of literature (see definition given under the discussion of Eze 37:1-14).[7] All characteristics of this literary genre are present in Ezekiel 40-48: (1) the passage was written under exilic conditions; (2) it is prophetic literature; (3) the theological thrust is eschatological; (4) the passage concerns a vision (40:2) and symbolism is present (chap. 43); and (5) there is a divine guide and interpreter (cf. 40:3). The setting of the vision (with the date, situation, and recipient) is found in 40:1-4, while the content of the vision itself is revealed in the remainder of these chapters. The interpretation is inter-mixed with the vision scenes.

The recognition that these nine chapters encompass a single apoc-alyptic vision is significant: (1) It demonstrates that this is a separate section of Ezekiel and an entity in and of itself. It is not a continuation of the previous chapters and their argument, but it begins a new discus-sion, though not totally unrelated to the rest of the development of the book. (2) It helps the interpreter to know how to properly interpret these chapters.[8]

SUMMARY

Ezekiel 40-48 forms the grand finale to this magnificent book. The book began with Ezekiel receiving a vision of God's sublime glory on the plain beside the river Chebar (chap. 1). That vision was a mag-

---

7. Cf. Ralph H. Alexander "Hermeneutics of Old Testament Apocalyptic Litera-ture," pp. 12-45.
8. Ibid., pp. 108-261.

nificent manifestation of the God of Israel who had resided with His people in their Temple from their inception (cf. Ex 40:34-35). Reflecting upon the majestic nature of Almighty God, Ezekiel was better able to understand the nature of his ministry—a ministry of judgment and promise—to the exiles in Babylon. This was the same glorious God who disciplined Israel for breaking His Mosaic covenant with her. Because she continually disobeyed God's laws, God chastened her and withdrew His glory from her (chaps. 8, 10, 11). Jerusalem had fallen and the nation had gone into captivity to Babylon. Then Ezekiel announced Israel's hope of restoration to the land of Israel and the Kingdom blessings in the Millennium. Thirteen years after Ezekiel proclaimed the hope of ultimate restoration, he solidified that hope with a detailed apocalyptic vision describing the nature of the millennial Kingdom. However, this vision does not describe all facets of the Millennium, but only the return of the glory of God and its attendant blessings. Just as the glory of God departed from Israel in order that judgment might be enacted, so after the completion of that cursing, the glory of God will return to dwell with His people.

The residence of God's glory in Israel's past has been the tabernacle and then the Temple. It will also be necessary for a Temple to be constructed in the millennial Kingdom to provide a dwelling place for the returning glory of God. Ezekiel 40-42 describes in detail the plans for such a Temple. The return of the glory of God to that Temple to dwell with Israel forever is portrayed in 43:1-12. Since under the Mosaic covenant Israel had failed to keep the properly ordained worship functions of the Temple and its priests, God charges the people of Israel to perform the new rituals of the Millennium in an unerring manner. In doing so, they will demonstrate that their lives have been changed (43:10-11; 44:5-8). Finally Israel will obey God's regulations, something she never did previously. In 43:13—46:24 are enumerated the requirements and functions of the priests, princes, and people as they participate in the worship of Yahweh and the commemoration of His glorious person and work. Yahweh will be dwelling with His people again; He will do so forever.

Ezekiel 47 and 48 show the manifestation of the blessing of God within the Temple as it outwardly affects the entire land of Israel. God reveals how the source of blessing and refreshment for the physical land of Israel issues forth from His glorious presence in the Temple through a supernatural stream, just as it did in the Garden of Eden (Gen 2:9-10) and as it will do in the eternal state (Rev 22:1-3). Then the millennial borders of the tribes of Israel are delineated. Concluding the book is a most profound assertion: the name of the city (Jerusalem) from that day forward will be *Yahweh-shammah,* "Yahweh is there!" He is there! He will *never* again withdraw His glory from Israel! He *will* be in their midst forever and ever throughout eternity!

The literary form of apocalyptic literature was followed closely by Ezekiel. The description of the setting of the vision was recounted in 40:1-4, while the content of the vision was portrayed in 40:5—48:35.

THE SETTING OF THE APOCALYPTIC VISION (40:1-4)

Four elements normally comprise the setting of an apocalyptic vision: (1) the date, (2) the identity of the recipient, (3) the location of the reception of the vision, and (4) noteworthy circumstances under which the vision was received. In this apocalyptic vision, the date is stated four different ways in 40:1.

First, Ezekiel employed his normal calendrical system of dating in reference to the deportation of Jehoiachin into exile (cf. 1:1-3). This vision was received in the twenty-fifth year of the captivity, or 573 B.C.

Second, this vision was received in the first of the year. Since Israel had both a civil calendar, which began in the fall, and a religious calendar, which began in the spring, expositors have interpreted this statement as referring to the spring of the new year in the month of Nisan (Mar./Apr.) or to the fall of the new year in the month of Tishri (Sept./Oct.). Since Ezekiel, a priest, was concerned about ecclesiastical affairs, especially in the vision of these chapters, it would seem more appropriate to select the spring religious calendar and therefore date the vision in March/April, 573 B.C.

Third, the tenth day of the month was specified: the tenth day of Nisan. The vision was received on the very day that Israel was required to begin preparation for the Passover. On this commencement of the commemoration of God's deliverance of His people from Egypt, a continual picture lesson of His ultimate redemption for them, God revealed the hope of the future Messianic blessings and worship which Israel will experience because of the Messiah's redemptive work.

Finally, Ezekiel declared that the vision was received in the fourteenth year after Jerusalem was destroyed. The fall of Jerusalem in 586 B.C. was a visible culmination of God's discipline of Israel for her disobedience to His covenant as well as a vindication of Ezekiel's prophetic ministry. Now, by contrast, the erection of a millennial Temple and its attendant worship are equally a culmination of God's program for Israel and a confirmation of Ezekiel's prophecies of hope delivered thirteen years previously (cf. 33:22).

The second element of the setting is the identity of the recipient. Though the name Ezekiel is not explicitly employed, the abundant use of the first person pronoun in light of the entire context of the book leaves no doubt that the recipient is Ezekiel.

The third aspect of this introduction declares that Ezekiel saw the events in the vision in the land of Israel upon a very high mountain where he was viewing the structure of a city (Jerusalem) from the north (40:2). The high mountain is not identified. With all of the geographical changes that transpire prior to the Millennium (Zec 14; Rev 6-19), one cannot be certain of this unidentified location. The implications from within the vision—associating the Temple with the same vicinity as the city—may tend to favor Mount Zion. However, the exact location where Ezekiel was when he received the vision is not stated.

The last aspect of the setting involves noteworthy circumstances under which the vision transpired. Ezekiel observed a divine messenger, carrying a measuring rod and measuring cord, who would be his guide and interpreter throughout the vision. This messenger exhorted Ezekiel to give attention to all that he would see and hear, for he would be required to declare it to the house of Israel (40:4).

THE CONTENT OF THE VISION (40:5—48:35)

The vision is divided into four distinct segments by common introductory formulas employed by Ezekiel (e.g., "behold," "and he brought me," and "thus saith the Lord [Yahweh]") and by subject matter: (1) the description of the millennial Temple area (40:5—42:20); (2) the

137

account of the return of the glory of God to the Temple (43:1-9); (3) the Temple regulations (43:10—46:24); and (4) the geographical characteristics of the land of Israel in the Millennium (47:1—48:35).

THE DESCRIPTION OF THE TEMPLE AREA (40:5—42:20)

The detailed architectural plans in these chapters are sufficient for architects to draw plans and reconstruct models with a fair degree of accuracy. Floor plans are given, but there are few notations about the dimensions and design of the superstructure.

Much has been said in seeking to ascertain the exact length of a cubit. Archaeological data has been sparse with respect to implements of measure in the ancient Near East. Likewise, linear measurements were determined by parts of the body, which vary with each individual. The cubit is measured from the tip of the middle finger to the point of the elbow. The palm, or handbreadth, is taken from the width of the hand at the base of the fingers. Therefore, the palm is about three inches, whereas the cubit, being equal to six palms, is estimated at approximately eighteen inches. One can read of "royal cubits," "long cubits," and "short cubits," but minute precision is absurd in light of the nature of the measurement. Ezekiel 40:5 and 43:13 indicate that Ezekiel's cubit is the length of a normal cubit plus a palm, implying that there is a standard cubit shorter than that which he employed. Most expositors, therefore, understand Ezekiel's cubit to be the normal eighteen-inch cubit plus a handbreadth of three inches: a total length of approximately twenty-one inches. As measurements are noted in these two chapters and in this commentary, consult the Appendix for the basic dimensional equivalents in feet.

The different aspects of the Temple complex are treated from the exterior to the interior, concluding with a summary (42:15-20) of the overall structure: (1) the outer court (40:5-26); (2) the inner court (40:27-31, 47); (3) accessories for the courts (40:38-46); (4) the Temple structure and the western building of the yard of separation (40:48—41:26); and (5) the priests' chambers (42:1-14). There is an abundance of details concerning this complex which undoubtedly demonstrates that God means for it to be constructed. This is an encouragement to the exiles in Babylon (cf. 43:10-11). As the varying

Fig. 1. Temple Complex

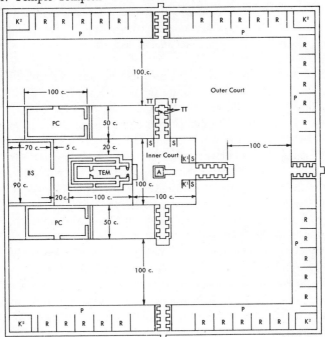

KEY

A   Altar (Eze 40:47**b**)

BS   Building of separation yard (Eze 41:12-13b, 15)

K¹   Kitchens for priests to boil sacrifices (Eze 46:19-20)

K²   Kitchens for priests to boil people's sacrifices (Eze 46:21-24)

P   Pavement (Eze 40:17-18)

PC   Priests' chambers (Eze 42:1-14)

R   Rooms in outer court for storage or priests (Eze 40:17)

S   Rooms for singers (priests) (Eze 40:44-46)

TT   Tables for slaughter of sacrifices (Eze 40:39-43)

TEM Temple proper (Eze 40:48—41:11, 13a, 14, 16, 23-26)

     Inner court (Eze 40:4-7a)

     Outer court (Eze 40:17-19, 23, 27, 39-43)

     Width from outer gates to inner gates (Eze 40:19, 23, 27)

features of the Temple area are described in the text and discussed in this commentary, continually consult figures 1 through 4. Much of the text is self-explanatory as the passage is compared with the visual ground plans. These are simply architectural specifications; hidden truths are not to be found in them.

The outer court (40:5-26). Comment on the outer court of the complex (see fig. 1) begins by stating the measurements of the wall surrounding the complex: one rod wide and one rod high (40:5). The remaining verses treat the design of the gate system which pertains to each of the three outer gates: one to the east (40:6-16), one to the north (40:20-23), and one to the south (40:24-26), respectively. The gate systems are very similar to the three and four entryway gates common to the fortified cities from the time of the united kingdom under David and Solomon to Ezekiel's day. The description is easy to follow if one observes figure 2 as he reads the biblical text of this section.

Ezekiel's tour of the Temple complex begins at the east gate. This gate is the most important gate since the glory of God will return through it, and the prince shall minister in it (cf. 43:1-9; 44:3).

Variant readings are found in many of the newer translations which create confusion where it is unnecessary. Words and numbers are often altered, though this is needless throughout these chapters. If there should be a textual change, one must have good reasons for it rather than his subjective desires.

The three outer gates have identical measurements. Symmetry is important and prevalent in these blueprints. In observing the descriptions of God's Messianic Temple, it is clear that He is a God of order and beauty.

A brief statement is given in 40:17-19 concerning some general features of the outer court. Thirty rooms are spaced evenly on the north, east, and south sides of the courtyard with a pavement in front of them (cf. fig. 1). The space between the outer and inner gates on either side of the outer court is one hundred cubits.

The inner court. The inner court is characterized primarily by its gate systems which are identical in dimensions to the outer court gates with one notable difference: the porches are located at the outer side of the gate toward the outer court rather than on the inward side of the gate,

Fig. 2. Gate System for All Gates of the Outer Court

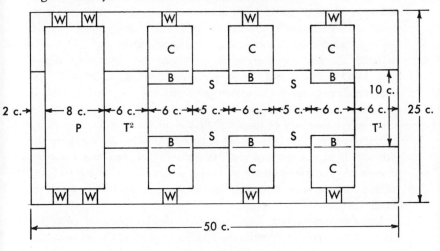

KEY

B	Borders (barriers, space) (Eze 40:12a)
C	Chambers (side rooms, guard rooms) (Eze 40:7a, 10a)
P	Porch (vestibule) (Eze 40:7c, 8-10b, 14)
S	Space between chambers (Eze 40:7b, 12b)
T¹	Threshold of the gate (Eze 40:6, 11)
T²	Threshold of the porch (Eze 40:7c)
W	Windows (Eze 40:16)
	Overall height, length, and width of the gate (Eze 40:13-15)

as in the outer court gates (cf. 40:31). In addition, the outer gates have only seven steps leading up to them, whereas the inner gates have eight (40:31). The progression of describing the inner gates moves from the south gate counterclockwise to the north one.

Next, the auxiliary items in the inner court are delineated. Tables for the slaughter of specified offerings are located both in the porch of the northern inner gate and also outside of that gate on either side. There are eight tables altogether: four inside and four outside (40:39-43; cf. fig. 1, T). There are three small rooms for the priestly singers on the inside of the northern inner gate and the eastern inner gate (40:44-46; cf. fig. 1, S). Two rooms are at the north gate and one at the east gate (vv. 44-45). The priests who keep the functions of the house of God also use these rooms. A singular room with the door facing north is located at the east inner gate for the sons of Zadok, the priests who carry on the functions of the altar. Ezekiel 40:47 gives the dimensions of the inner court as one hundred square cubits. This must refer to the area of the inner courtyard east (or in front) of the Temple proper. This would agree with all the other specifications. The altar mentioned in this same verse must refer to the altar for sacrifice further described in 43:13-17.

The Temple structure. The structure of the Temple itself (40:48—41:11, 13a, 14, 16, 23-26) and the building in front of the separate area to the west of the Temple (41:12-13b, 15) are described next. Ezekiel was guided through the Temple from the porch to the Holy of Holies (40:48—41:4). All dimensions are clear (cf. fig. 3), with perhaps the exception of 41:3. The entry to the Holy of Holies is described in this verse. The small two cubit pilasters are measured first, then a simple statement "and the entrance, six cubits" (ASV) is given. Since the width is given as seven cubits, the measurement of six cubits has been confusing. This measurement probably refers to the dimension of the sides of the entry in a parallel manner to the description of the entry to the Temple proper described in verse 2.

The "height" mentioned in 41:8 is the height of the side chambers, not the entire house of God. The dimension of twenty cubits in verse 10 must refer to the entire distance from the inside of the wall enclosing the holy place to the outside of the foundation space. The con-

142

Fig. 3. The Plan of the Temple Sanctuary

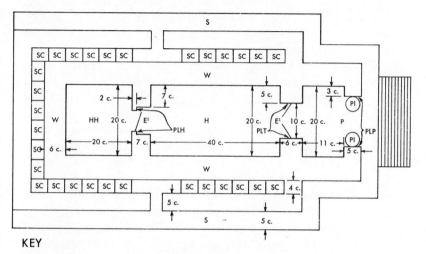

KEY

E¹	Entry to the Temple (Eze 41:2a; cf. 41:23-25)
E²	Entry to the Holy of Holies (Eze 41:3; cf. 41:23-25)
H	Holy Place (sanctuary) (Eze 41:2b, 21b)
HH	Holy of Holies (Eze 41:4)
P	Porch (vestibule) (Eze 40:48-49)
PI	Pillars (Eze 40:49)
PLH	Pilaster (jamb, post) of the entry to the Holy of Holies (Eze 41:3-4)
PLP	Pilaster of the porch (Eze 40:48)
PLT	Pilaster of the Temple proper (Eze 41:1)
SC	Side chambers of the Temple sanctuary (Eze 41:5b-11a)
S	Space left (platform) around the Temple (Eze 41:11b)
W	Wall of the house (Eze 41:5a)
	Overall dimensions of the Temple with yard on either side (Eze 41:13a, 14)
	Windows (Eze 41:16, 26) on the porch and side chambers and decorations (Eze 41:16-20)

text of verses 5 through 11 argues for this, as well as the combined measurements of the inner wall (6 cubits; cf. v. 5), the width of the side chambers (4 cubits; cf. v. 5), and the width of the outer wall (5 cubits; cf. v. 9), and the width of the space of the foundation (5 cubits; cf. v. 11) which add up to twenty cubits.

Ezekiel 41:12-15 alternates back and forth in its statements of the overall measurements of the building to the west of the Temple and those of the Temple itself. Verse 12 mentions the inner width and length of this building west of the separation (or yard) which lies between that building and the Temple. Verse 13 gives the length of the "house" or Temple (100 cubits) and the dimension from the western wall of the Temple proper to the western wall of the entire complex (100 cubits including the yard of separation, the western building and its walls on both sides). The measurement of the width of the inner courtyard, as one faces the front of the Temple, with the yard of separation on either side is one hundred cubits. Verse 15 demonstrates that the length of the western building of the separation, with its walls and passageways is also one hundred cubits, which is identical to the width of the inner court. Undoubtedly all of these one hundred-cubit measurements were designed to show the symmetry of the whole (cf. fig. 3).

The decorations of the Temple structure, both inside and out, include wood panel wainscoting from the ground to the windows with palm tree and cherubim designs upon it (41:16-20). This decoration was to be used both on the inside and on the outside of the Temple, as well as on the doors of the Temple and of the Holy of Holies (41:17-26). Narrow windows were built for the porch and the thirty side chambers of this three-story building (41:16, 23-26). The only piece of furniture mentioned in the Temple is an altar of wood called "the table that is before [Yahweh]" (41:22). By comparing dimensions, it is evident that this is not the altar of sacrifice (cf. 41:22 and 43:13-17). Some think that it may be an altar of incense.

Chambers for the priests. These chambers are to be constructed on either side of the inner court. They are actually located in the outer court and face north and south, respectively (cf. fig. 1, PC). The northern chamber is described in detail (42:1-9), and the southern chamber is then likened to it (42:10-12). The descriptions are a bit complicated in places. These chambers are one hundred cubits long (east to west) and fifty cubits wide (north to south) (vv. 2, 8). A step (not a walk) of ten cubits in width and one cubit in length is before the doorway on the north (v. 4; cf. v. 12). The buildings are three stories high, and each higher level is smaller in overall dimensions in order to make the building more structurally sound (vv. 5-6). Enclosure walls are to be built east of these chambers parallel to their width of fifty cubits (v. 7). These walls may provide privacy for the rooms. The door also is located on the east side (v. 9).

Verses 10-12 describe an identical building on the south side of the Temple. The Hebrew (v. 10), however, is normally rendered "east." The symmetry of the Temple complex, plus the explicit statement in verse 13 that the buildings are on the north and south, argue that "south" is a better reading of the text than "east."

These chambers provide the priests a place to eat their prescribed portions of the offerings and also give them a dressing room in which they can change from their ministry garments to civilian clothes (vv. 13-14).

This section which describes the Temple complex concludes with the guiding angel taking Ezekiel out through the east gate to observe the enormity of the area set apart for the entire Temple precinct. Each side of the area is equal: 500 rods on the east, north, south, and west. Some translations and some expositors immediately reject the term "rods" (or "reeds") and replace it with what they feel is the more suitable term, "cubit." The large majority of manuscripts and versions have the word "cubit" instead of "rod." However, to exchange these terms is not in keeping with 45:2, where the Temple environs are measured as 500 square. Though neither rods nor cubits are explicitly stated in that context, the next phrase declares that there is to be a fifty-*cubit* open space around this 500 square area. It appears that Ezekiel had explicitly employed the word "cubit" at this point to distinguish it from 500 "rods" as revealed in the passage at hand (40:15-20). Likewise, the main argument for changing the reading to "cubits" is that it supposedly will fit the existing topography better. Yet Zechariah 14 and other passages clearly demonstrate that enormous geographical modifications will transpire at the beginning of the Millennium. No one knows the exact topography that will be in existence in the Millennium. Therefore this writer sees no reason to alter the term "rods."

A wall is said to be around the entire area. This is not the wall mentioned in Ezekiel 40:5, which was the one connecting the three outer gates. The wall mentioned in this context is around the entire Temple region. Most important of all is the last statement of 42:20: This wall and area are to separate the holy Temple area from the sinfulness of man. God desires that the Jews recognize the distinction between the holy and the profane. Though their past history demonstrates that they were not able to make that distinction, in the Messianic Kingdom that distinction will be extremely clear.

THE PORTRAYAL OF THE RETURN OF THE GLORY OF GOD TO THE TEMPLE (43:1-9)

The most significant event in these nine chapters is the return of the glory of God to the Temple. The whole argument and unity of the book is consummated in this act. Then the millennial Temple, which has been architecturally described, will be dedicated in a manner similar to the dedication of the tabernacle (Ex 40:34-35) and Solomon's Temple (1 Ki 8:10-11; 2 Ch 5:13-14; 7:1-3); the glory of God will fill the Temple.

Certainly this vision stirred the heart of Ezekiel and those who received it from him, for some could still remember the glories of the Temple of Solomon (cf. Hag 2:3). But the people of Israel were being disciplined. Yahweh had withdrawn His glory from their presence and from the Temple in Jerusalem (cf. the visions in Eze 8, 10, 11) in order to bring the present judgment upon His people to cleanse them from their abominations. The glory of God would not fill a temple structure again until the fulfillment of this present vision, not even the reconstruction of the Temple during the time of restoration under Zerubbabel (cf. Ezra 6 and Hag 2:7, 9).

Ezekiel saw God's glory, the glory of the God of Israel (v. 3), the glory of Yahweh (v. 4), the same glory before which he fell in awe on the banks of the river Chebar (cf. chap. 1) and which he saw depart from Jerusalem in preparation for that city's destruction (43:3; cf. chaps. 10, 11). In the vision Ezekiel witnessed God's glory return to the house of God through the east gate, just as it had left the Temple in 10:18 and 11:22.[9] The accompanying sound as of "many waters" reminded him of the familiar noise of the cherubims' wings (1:24).

The divine interpretation of this vision begins in verse 6. Yahweh spoke to Ezekiel from the Temple; Ezekiel's guide-interpreter stood beside him. This message was so important that Yahweh delivered it Himself: It is "the place of my throne, . . . I will dwell in the midst of the children of Israel for ever" (43:7)! The discipline is over! The glory of Yahweh has returned to dwell with His people! The promises of chapters 33-37 are true!

Yahweh continued to explain the significance of His return in verses 7-9. Israel had defiled Yahweh's holy name by her previous abominations, but now she will never again do so (cf. 39:7). The Lord's instructions for the use of this new Temple are to be seen in the light of His glorious presence. These precepts form the second part of God's speech to Ezekiel which are treated separately as the "Temple Regulations."

TEMPLE REGULATIONS (43:10—46:24)

Ezekiel 43:10-11 serves as a transition at this juncture. The glory of God had just returned during the dedication of the new Temple. Israel was exhorted by Yahweh to be ashamed of her past iniquities. The holiness of God always puts the sin of man in extreme contrast. Since Israel's past sins had been cleansed (cf. chaps. 36-37), now the holiness and glory of God could be present. Consequently, Israel, in the Millennium, is to follow Yahweh's holy and righteous ways. Yahweh commanded Ezekiel to set forth these ways in written form in order that Israel might know and keep them. The purpose of these laws and statutes was to instruct Israel in the worship of Yahweh in true holiness.

The section is divided into two parts. First, Ezekiel recorded the regulations for the structures of the Temple complex: the proper respect of the Temple precinct (43:12), the pattern and dedication of the altar of sacrifice (43:13-27), and the function and use of the east gate (44:1-3). Following a brief exhortation to perform the worship of the Temple

---

9. It is interesting to observe that Jesus left and will return to Jerusalem in a similar manner (cf. Ac 1 and Zec 14).

Fig. 4. Altar of Sacrifice

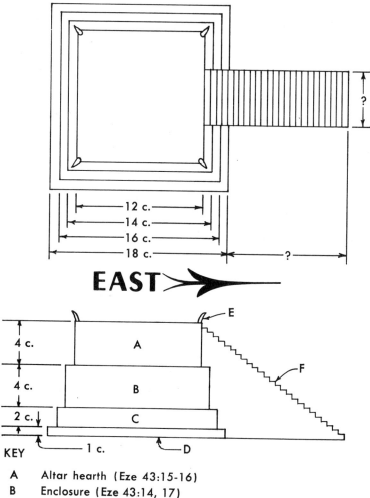

KEY

A   Altar hearth (Eze 43:15-16)
B   Enclosure (Eze 43:14, 17)
C   Interior (Eze 43:14, 17)
D   Bottom (Eze 43:13)
E   Horns of the altar (Eze 43:15)
F   Steps (Eze 43:17)

148

correctly (44:4-8), Yahweh set forth the statutes for the conduct of worship: the regulations of the priesthood (44:9-31); the holy contribution of land for the priests, the sanctuary, and Jerusalem (45:1-8); the functions of the princes of Israel (45:9-17); the liturgical calendar (45:18-25); the worship of the prince and the people (46:1-15); the bequest of the prince's inheritance (46:16-18); and the description of the boiling rooms for sacrifices (46:19-24).

The law of the house (43:12). This law emphasized the holiness of the Temple area, separated upon the top of the mountain. The boundaries of separation must be maintained.

The design and dedication of the altar of sacrifice (43:13-27). The measurements of this altar demonstrated that its shape is similar to the altar in the tabernacle and in the Solomonic Temple (cf. 2 Ch 4:1), but is smaller (vv. 13-17; cf. fig. 4). Though all the features described may not be understood, the basic design is plain.[10]

Next, Yahweh described the dedicatory procedures (the "statutes" of the altar, NASB) for the altar of sacrifice (vv. 18-27). The Levitical priests of the descendants of Zadok are to officiate. The altar is to be cleansed and consecrated (cf. Ex 29:36-37; 2 Ch 7:9) with sin offerings made on the first two days (a young bull and then a young he goat) (43:19-22). When the altar is cleansed, it is consecrated with a burnt offering of a young bull and he goat (vv. 23-24). The cleansing and consecration will last seven days (vv. 25-26), after which the people may then bring their voluntary burnt offerings and peace offerings. A wonderful promise is given in verse 27. Not only will their sacrifices be accepted, but Yahweh will likewise accept the offerers.

The function of the east gate (44:1-3). The function of the east gate of the outer court (cf. 40:6-16) relates primarily to the prince. This is the same gate through which the glory of Yahweh entered this millennial Temple in 43:1-4. In reverence and sanctity of that event, this gate will be closed (v. 2). There is a popular idea that the present "golden gate" of Jerusalem, which is sealed, is the gate mentioned in this passage. This, however, cannot be the case since the dimensions of the two com-

10. It is interesting to compare the exhortation concerning steps of the altar in Ex 20:24-26 with this text.

plexes are different and the present-day structures will be replaced by the millennial ones.

The prince will be an exception to the principle set forth in verse 2. Though he will not go through the east gate,[11] he will be permitted to eat bread before Yahweh in its porch. Who is this prince? He is not the Messiah. He is said to "eat bread before [Yahweh]" (44:3). If he were Yahweh, this would be contradictory. In addition, he is to make sin offerings for the people and also for himself (45:22). Though it is understood that the offerings in the Millennium are commemorative and not expiatory, they do commemorate the necessity of Christ's death as a sin offering for sinfulness. The implication, then, is that the prince is one whose sinfulness has been forgiven by Christ's death. If that is true, he most certainly could not be the Messiah. Last, the prince has children (46:16), which is impossible if he is the Messiah.

Since the prince is a man, many have sought to identify him with the historical David, seeking support from the texts of 34:23-24 and 37:24. It has already been demonstrated that those texts most clearly refer to the Messiah, not the historical David. Actually, the prince's identity is unknown. He functions as a vice-regent of Yahweh in the Messianic Kingdom.

An exhortation to holy worship (44:4-8). This exhortation is delivered through Ezekiel to the rebellious house of Israel. As Ezekiel was brought again to view the glory of God filling the Temple, Yahweh reminded the exiles of their abominable practices of worship, practices that were performed in direct disobedience to Yahweh's revealed Word. His people had allowed the foreigners and the uncircumcised in the Temple, and they had not placed Yahweh's appointees in charge of the Temple duties. In contrast, Yahweh will demonstrate how He is to be worshiped properly by setting forth regulations for the millennial Temple worship.

Regulations for the priesthood (44:9-31). These regulations begin by declaring that only the Levites shall minister in Yahweh's sanctuary. No foreigners and no uncircumcised person, either in the flesh or the heart, will be allowed in the sanctuary (v. 9).

11. The prince approaches from the side of the outer court where the porch lies and he leaves from that same side (cf. 44:3 and 46:2, 8).

Among the Levites, there will be two divisions. All the Levites except the sons of Zadok will serve as overseers at the gate of the sanctuary (vv. 10-14). They will not serve by offering sacrifices because of their past sins of idolatry. In this sense, they will bear their past iniquities.

On the other hand, the sons of Zadok, who were faithful in following Yahweh's ways, even when the nation strayed from Him (cf. 1 Sa 2:35; 2 Sa 8:17; 15:24-29; 1 Ki 2:26-35; 1 Ch 6:7-8), will minister the holy things in the sanctuary (vv. 15-16). Explicit regulations are set forth for them. First, they are to wear only linen clothing when serving in the inner court and the sanctuary. If wool were worn, it would cause them to perspire, an indication of uncleanness (vv. 17-18). When they go out into the outer court among the people, they are to wear other garments. This is to portray the holiness and sanctity of Yahweh, His Temple, and His worship (v. 19; cf. 42:14). Second, they are not to shave their heads nor let their hair grow long (v. 20), both of which were signs of defilement in the Mosaic system (cf. Lev 10:6; 21:5, 10). Third, the sons of Zadok were not to partake of wine while ministering in the inner court lest they lose full control of their mental faculties (v. 21; cf. Lev 10:9). Fourth, the marriage to any woman except a virgin or a widow of a priest was forbidden (v. 22; cf. Lev 21:14). This type of regulation is found only for the high priest in the Mosaic system, but in the Millennium all priests will follow this rule. It emphasizes the purity and sanctity of God's holy things.

The foregoing regulations stress the need for holiness and cleanness among ministering priests. This emphasis is at the heart of the priestly functions outlined in verses 23-27, for they are to teach the distinction between the holy and profane (clean and unclean) (v. 23; cf. Lev 10:10; 11:47), to judge lawsuits of the people (v. 24a), to keep Yahweh's Law and statutes, especially the holy days and the Sabbaths (v. 24b), and to keep themselves from defilement, except when a family member dies, after which they must be cleansed according to proper procedures (vv. 25-27).

The regulations for the priesthood conclude by describing the provisions for the priests. Yahweh will be both their inheritance and their possession (instead of land, v. 28). Their daily provisions will be received from the people of Israel through sacrificial offerings and the

Fig. 5. Land Allotment in the Millennium

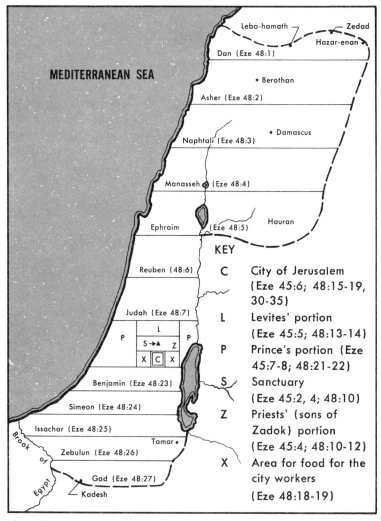

The allotments are only estimated since the Scripture is clear that major topographical changes will transpire prior to the Millennium. (See Eze 45:1-8; 47:13—48:35.)

firstfruits of the land (vv. 29-30), so long as they do not eat any torn animal or bird (v. 31).

The apportionment of the land of Israel during the Millennium (45:1-8). This apportionment arises out of the preceding discussion of the priests' inheritance in 44:28-31. An additional possession will belong to the priests in this future Kingdom: a portion of the land of Israel when it is divided (cf. 47:13—48:35).

The specific allotment is described as an offering to Yahweh, "an holy portion of the land" (v. 1). In other words, it really belongs to Yahweh, not to the priests. This agrees with the fact that Yahweh is their possession and inheritance (44:28). This land segment will measure 25,000 by 10,000. Though the text does not explicitly state that "rods" are the nature of the measurement, this certainly seems to be the case when one examines verse 2. The Temple precinct, which lies in the middle of this allotment, is measured 500 by 500 square. In contrast, the border around it is explicitly stated to be fifty cubits. The term "cubit" appears to be used purposefully to contrast the fifty measurements from the 500. Likewise, the same dimensions of the Temple complex are revealed in 42:15-20 as 500 "rods."

This 25,000 rod by 10,000 rod segment is only one of three parts that comprised this offering to Yahweh (cf. 48:9 and fig. 5). This specific portion is for the priests, the sons of Zadok, who draw near to Yahweh with the sacrifices (cf. 45:4 with 44:15-16; 48:10-12).

A second 25,000 rod by 10,000 rod area is set aside for the rest of the Levites, the ministers of the house (cf. 44:10-14; 48:13-14). This allotment lies north of the portion containing the sanctuary, for 48:8, 21 declares that the sanctuary is located in the middle of the entire 25,000 by 25,000 area between Judah and Benjamin. This would then mean that the priestly segment would be in the middle and the Levitical portion to the north, for the last allotment of the 25,000 rod by 5,000 rod area certainly appears to be on the south next to the inheritance of Benjamin (cf. 45:6; 48:15-19, 30-35). This last area is set aside for the city of Jerusalem and is an allotment for the whole house of Israel, that is, all the people have access to this part of the holy offering to Yahweh whereas the other portions are explicitly for the Levites and priests. Most likely the priestly segment is discussed first in this passage as well as in chapter 48 because of its holy importance rather than its geographical location.

In 45:7-8a (cf. 48:21) the portion of land set aside for the prince (cf. 44:1-3) is said to be the remaining area to the east and west of the 25,000-rod square area known as "the offering to Yahweh." Everything east to the Jordan River and west to the sea on either side of the "offering" belongs to the prince.

Finally, the remainder of the land is for the rest of Israel (45:8b). The manner of allotment is specifically described in 47:13—48:7; 48: 23-29.

The functions of the prince. The prince's functions constitute the final laws of the Temple (45:9—46:24; cf. 44:1-3). An interlude in which Yahweh spoke to the contemporary princes residing in the exile demonstrates, by contrast, the demand for a righteous rule in the Millennium (45:9-12). The present leadership of Israel had afflicted Yahweh's people (45:8a), becoming wealthy at their expense through violence and the deceit of illegal weights and measurements. (Correct measurements are outlined in 45:11-12; cf. 1 Ki 10:17; 2 Ch 9:16.)

In contrast to these unrighteous rulers, the functions of the righteous prince in the Millennium are outlined in 45:13—46:18. The fundamental task of the prince is to present the offerings for the people of Israel on the appointed holy days (45:17). The people will provide the wheat, barley, oil, and lambs in proper proportions for the meal offerings, burnt offerings, peace offerings, and sin offerings (45:13-16; cf. 46:13-15), which the prince, in turn, will offer to Yahweh as a memorial (45:17). Again, these millennial offerings are not efficacious; they are only memorials.

A calendar of appointed holy days and feasts during which the prince will make offerings is set forth in 45:18—46:15. First, the prince is responsible to offer sacrifices for the cleansing of the sanctuary on the first and seventh days of the first month of the religious calendar, the month of Nisan (equivalent to our Mar./Apr.; 45:18-20). The prince is the responsible official, represented by the singular verb of 45:18. The priest, however, aids the prince by actually performing the ritual of the offering in the sanctuary (v. 19). Second, the prince makes a sin offering for himself and the people on the first day of Passover (Nisan

14) and offers daily prescribed offerings for the seven days of unleavened bread (vv. 21-24). Third, the prince observes the Feast of Tabernacles with its appointed offerings on the fifteenth day of the seventh month (Tishri, equivalent to Sept./Oct.; v. 25). Fourth, 46:1-11 sets forth the correct procedure and offerings for the Sabbath and new moons. On the Sabbath the prince is to worship at the inner threshold of the east gate of the inner court. Here the priests prepare his offerings (vv. 2, 4-7, 8, 11). The people worship at the outer entrance of that same gate (v. 3). The orderly flow of these worshipers is prescribed in verses 9 and 10. On the remaining six days that gate is to be closed (v. 1). Fifth, the procedure which the prince follows for making freewill offerings is stated in 46:12.

Besides these religious functions of the prince, guidelines for dispersing his inheritance are outlined in 46:16-18. The inheritance of the prince's son is permanent. A gift from his inheritance to a servant is retained only until the year of Jubilee (49 years). Then it must be returned. This millennial prince will never oppress the people by taking their inheritance from them, as did the princes of Israel in the time of Ezekiel (45:18).

Finally, an appendix concludes this section in which the various kitchens of the priests are described (46:19-24). Kitchens are located in the inner court (cf. fig. 1, K¹) for the boiling and baking of the offerings, probably the daily ritual offerings (vv. 19-20). The exact location of these kitchens is disputed, though it seems that they are located next to the eastern inner gate (cf. 40:46). Additional kitchens are found in the four corners of the outer court, specifically designed for the boiling of the people's offerings (cf. fig. 1. K²; 45:21-24).

THE GEOGRAPHICAL CHARACTERISTICS OF THE LAND OF ISRAEL IN THE MILLENNIUM (47:1—48:35).

It seems appropriate to conclude this prophecy with a discussion of the land of Israel during the Millennium. The land of Canaan has played an integral role in the history of God's people. It was first mentioned in the promise of God to Abraham (Gen 12:7). In the Mosaic covenant the people of Israel were instructed that obedience to that covenant would bring blessing. One of the blessings appropriated was the land promise to Abraham (cf. Deu 7:12-13; 8:1). When Israel followed the Mosaic covenant they resided in the land of Palestine. However, due to their rebellion against God's Law, the Israelites presently found themselves as exiles in Babylon, removed from the land of blessing just as Ezekiel prophesied.

However, God has promised that He will restore His people to the land which He promised to give to them (Eze 36), and no one will ever be able to wrest it from them (cf. chaps. 38-39). It is theirs, and the way in which they will divide it is set forth now in these final chapters.

Two specific topics are treated in these two chapters. First, the river which heals the land is described in 47:1-12. Second, the tribal divisions of the land are defined in 47:13—48:35.

The river flowing from the Temple (47:1-12). The river is a literal river which is described as flowing eastward from the Temple to the Dead Sea, as well as to other undefined areas. The waters originate as a trickle (47:2) from the right side of the threshold of the Temple, flow past the south side of the altar and under the right side of the eastern outer gate of the Temple complex, progressively rising in depth (at 1,000-cubit intervals) from the ankles to the knees and then to a depth that demands that one swim (47:3-5). Lining the edges of this stream are many trees (47:6-7).

The purpose of this river and its trees is clearly stated as healing (47:8-12). The desert rift of the southern Jordan Valley south to the Red Sea (the Aravah), will be transformed into a blooming oasis where normal life can exist. The Dead Sea will come alive with swarms of every kind of fish like those found in the Mediterranean Sea. Everywhere the river goes there will be healing so that all will live. The leaves of the trees which cover the banks of the river will provide healing to the people, while their fruit will furnish food.

God has made the provisions for life in the Millennium dependent upon Him. Life flows from the throne of God, the Temple (43:7). Though this passage is not equivalent to a similar description in the eternal state (in Rev 22 as discussed previously), it does appear that the initial concept of blessing in this manner stems from the passage in Genesis 2:9-10. The source of God's blessings flow out from God, just

156

as the psalmist declares (Ps 46:4). According to Zechariah 14:8, a similar stream flows from the city of Jerusalem both to the east and to the west, providing blessing upon the land.

The tribal land divisions and borders (47:13—48:35). The divisions and borders for Israel in the Millennium are delineated in this closing section. First, the boundary which sets off the land area allotted to Israel is defined in detail, following known geographical place names from Ezekiel's day (47:13-20). It is assumed that similar locations and topography would be employed in the Millennium (cf. fig. 5). In this description the east sea is the same as the Dead Sea of Ezekiel's day.

Second, Yahweh commands that this area be divided among the tribes of Israel along with the sojourners and strangers who are living in her midst (47:21-23).

Third, a specific delineation of tribal areas within the general boundary set forth in 47:13-20 is charted geographically from north to south (48:1-29; cf. fig. 5). Proceeding from the north, the tribes are listed in order as Dan, Asher, Naphtali, Manasseh, Ephraim, Reuben, and Judah (48:1-7). It is assumed that the land portions are equal since no other data is given. South of these seven tribes lies the holy offering described in 45:1-8. Further information is given in 48:8-20 about each segment of this 25,000-square rod holy contribution to Yahweh, especially the common land which encompasses the city (48:15-20). The city, unnamed at this juncture, will be 4,500 rods square with a border of 250 rods around it on all sides. The result is a 5,000-square rod city area. The 10,000 by 5,000 rod area to the east and west of that city area will provide the food (bread) for the workers within the city (48:18-19; cf. fig. 5, X). The remainder of this north-south section which includes the holy offering to Yahweh—the areas to the east and west of the 25,000-square contribution—belong to the prince (48:21). The entire oblation is summarized in 48:22-23. Finally, the other five tribes of Israel are allotted territories to the south of this holy area in order: Benjamin, Simeon, Issachar, Zebulun, and Gad (48:24-29).

The final part of this section of the prophecy describes the city (48: 30-35). Most would identify this city as the city of Jerusalem (cf. Zec 14:8). Three facets of the city are discussed. First, there are twelve gates to the city, three on each side. The northern gates are named for the tribes of Reuben, Judah, and Levi (v. 31), while the eastern gates are named after the tribes of Joseph, Benjamin, and Dan (v. 32). Simeon, Issachar, and Zebulun give their names to the southern three gates (v. 33), while Gad, Asher, and Naphtali designate the gates on the west (v. 34). There is no known reason for this particular order of names, nor for the order of tribal divisions in 48:8-20. Neither order compares with the encampment of the tribes in the wilderness wanderings (cf. Num 2).

The second facet of this city is the measurement of its circumference: 18,000 rods (48:35*a*).

The last aspect of this section, and of the book, is most significant: the name of the city. The city will be known from that day forward as *Yahweh-shammah:* "Yahweh is there!" This name encompasses the major thrust of this final apocalyptic vision of the prophecy. Yahweh is present. He is with Israel; He will never leave them. His covenants are fulfilled!

APPENDIX

(Based on cubit of approximately 21 inches)

Cubits	Feet	Cubits	Feet
⅙	.25	13	22.75
(1 palm)	(3 inches)	14	24.50
1	1.75	15	26.25
2	3.50	16	28.00
3	5.25	20	35.00
4	7.00	25	43.75
5	8.75	40	70.00
6	10.50	50	87.50
(1 rod)		60	105.00
7	12.25	100	175.00
8	14.00	3,000	5,250.00
9	15.75	(500 rods)	(almost 1 mile)
10	17.50		
11	19.25		
12	21.00		

BIBLIOGRAPHY

Archer, Gleason L., Jr. *A Survey of Old Testament Introduction.* Rev. ed. Chicago: Moody, 1974.

Cooke, George A. *A Critical and Exegetical Commentary on the Book of Ezekiel.* The International Critical Commentary, ed. S. R. Driver, A. Plummer, and C. A. Briggs. Edinburgh: T. & T. Clark, 1936.

Ellison, Henry L. *Ezekiel: The Man and His Message.* Grand Rapids: Eerdmans, 1956.

Feinberg, Charles Lee. *The Prophecy of Ezekiel: The Glory of the Lord.* Chicago: Moody, 1969.

Freeman, Hobart E. *An Introduction to the Old Testament Prophets.* Chicago: Moody, 1972.

Gaebelein, A. C. *The Prophet Ezekiel, An Analytical Exposition.* New York: Our Hope, 1918.

Gray, James M. *Christian Workers' Commentary on the Old and New Testaments.* New York: Revell, 1915.

Keil, Carl F. *Biblical Commentary on Ezekiel.* 2 vols. Grand Rapids: Eerdmans, n.d.

Oppenheim, A. Leo. *The Interpretation of Dreams in the Ancient Near East with a Translation of an Assyrian Dream-Book.* Philadelphia: Amer. Phil. Soc., 1956.

Taylor, John B. *Ezekiel.* Tyndale Old Testament Commentaries, ed. D. J. Wiseman. Downers Grove, Ill.: Inter-Varsity, 1969.

Unger, Merrill F. *Great Neglected Bible Prophecies.* Wheaton, Ill.: Scripture Press, 1955.